You can order extra copies of this book:

Dynamic Media Publishing
www.mediacentresmadeeasy.com

Contact info:
Adam Szuster
C/o Dynamic Media Publishing
16 Shepherd Ct
Coromandel Valley
SA, Australia, 5051

ISBN   **978-0-9874514-1-5** (print)
        978-0-9874514-0-8 (ebook)

Preface

Being an avid consumer of media – particularly music and movies – it has always been important to find better ways of listening to and watching media. In this quest we end up with a range of different devices and machines - and their remotes. This quest is where I discovered media centres.

My first media centre began with a question. More precisely the same question, over and over and over again. It was this:

"Which buttons on which remotes do I need to push to watch TV [you can substitute DVD, Music, etc...]?"

The question led to the answer – a media centre. It enabled my wife to be able to watch TV using one remote. And it stopped the phone calls at work.

As my family did, you will find that a Media Centre changes the way you consume media. It will give you control over what you watch, how you watch and when you watch your movies, TV shows and music that interest you.

So I have written this book to help you with your quest to build the perfect media centre. In it you will find:

- step by step instructions on building a media centre
- step by step instructions on configuring your media centre
- pictures to guide you each step of the way
- information to help you decide which components to use
- ideas on what apps and plugins you can use to heighten your experience

You like to tinker; you like to build: so this book is designed to guide you through the process of building your very own media centre.

At the end of the book you will end up with a fully functional media centre that you can say, hand on heart, you built.

This is a reference book. Keep it with you as you build your media centre. Make notes in it. Refer to it.

It's that kind of book :)

Adam Szuster
ASENT Home Theatre Systems

CONTENTS

Part 1 – Hardware

Part 2 – The Build

Part 3 – Software

Part 4 – Media Center Plugins

Windows Media Center

XBMC

:: Introduction

We live in a digital world. Virtually all our media can now be consumed digitally – in fact, it is the preferred method by a large portion of our society.

Just think about music. No-one uses cassette tapes these days (remember those!). Even CDs are now going the way of the video recorder. Just about everyone listens to music on their MP3 player, be it an iPod, their mobile phone, or a dedicated MP3 player. It is expected that 2012 will be the year in which we see downloaded music overtake CD sales.

Movies are also heading in the same direction. Like the music industry, the movie houses have resisted the desire by consumers to buy movies in digital formats. And like the music industry the writing is on the wall. Some Blu-ray discs now come with downloadable versions of movies which can be stored on your computer, or digital media player, for personal viewing.

Even TV is predominantly digital in format now. Most European and North American countries have now completely switched off their analogue TV signals, with many others countries (like Australia, New Zealand, and the UK) to complete the transition in 2013.

The downside of this process of digitisation has been the proliferation of devices in the home. It is not uncommon to walk into a house and see the following:

Digital TV
Set top box
DVD/Blu-ray player
Digital receiver (and amplifier)
iPod dock

All these devices need remotes – so we are now in a position where we need several remotes just to watch the evening news!

A Media Centre (MC), also known as a Home Theatre PC (HTPC), changes all of this. A media centre consolidates all your digital media into one device that works with your TV and/or digital receiver. Now, all your digital TV, DVDs, CDs, Blu-rays, MP3s, internet radio stations, and digital photos can be stored, viewed and/or listened to, on a single system.

It's not hard to imagine the following scenario:

> *You invite some friends over for a dinner party and set your media centre to play a playlist of your favourite music (or stream an internet radio station) whilst showing a collection of relevant digital photos. After the meal, you all then sit around and watch the latest Blu-ray movie.*

This book will show you how to build your own media centre. It breaks down the seemingly complex task of building and configuring the media centre into four fundamental sections:

1.   Working out what you need
2.   Building the physical machine
3.   Installing and configuring the software
4.   Adding extra functionality with the power of add-ons and plugins

This book addresses the two most powerful media centre applications – Windows Media Centre and XBMC.

It investigates the pros and cons of each and then delves into setting up each one.

Now, you might be thinking:

Anything I read in this book is already out of date – technology moves very quickly and computer components are upgraded almost monthly.

And you'd be right.

So instead of telling you what items and components to use, this book demystifies component specifications, explains what they mean, and shows you what to look for when buying computer hardware. It also provides suggestions on which brands to seek out to ensure that your media centre experience is the best it can be.

The next section provides step-by-step instructions on building your very own media centre. This includes the all-important software installation and configuration process. Each step comes with a screen grab so that you can see exactly what is happening – and then compare that with what you are seeing on your very own system, so you can be sure that you are getting it right.

When you have finished reading the book, and have followed the instructions, you will have your very own working media centre that will be able to play all of your digital media.

Perfect!

So let's get started ...

Part 1

:: Hardware

Before we can build anything, we need to know what we are going to be building with – what components we will be using to make our perfect media centre. There are many differing opinions on what you should use. Some people say that you need the very best components. Others say that you can use an old, disused machine. The truth, in my experience, is somewhere in between.

Even people who have reasonable computer experience can be unclear on what they actually need. In this section of the book, we will look at the following questions:

> Exactly what parts do you need?
>
> Where should you spend a few extra dollars?
>
> More importantly: which parts can you afford to skimp on?

Part 1 will answer these questions and give you an idea on what parts to buy. However, I will not provide specific recommendations because components are developed and brought to market so rapidly, that whatever I tell you to use will be yesterday's news by the time you read this book.

So, in this section, you will find information on what, and what not, to look for. At the end of each topic, I have included a list of trusted brands that I have personally used to good effect. Their parts and components may change but their quality and reliability does not.

I will also include the specs of my very own personal system, which is surprisingly low-tech, to give you some idea about how low you can actually go.

:: Hardware Selection

Before you start building, we need to decide which parts you will use. This can be dictated by many factors, not the least of which is whether you will be using parts that you already have. If this is the case, it is worth reading this section because it will give you a guide to the minimum specs required for each of the sections. We will also be able to show you how to work out if what you already have is media centre applicable.

What we need to do is make a list of the items needed to make a media centre, so that we can then look at each in detail. So, what parts do we need to make a media centre?

Case

Motherboard

CPU

Power Supply

GPU

Tuner Cards

Hard Drives

RAM

Audio

Remote Controls

Networking

This might look like a list, however several of these items are now combined on the motherboard, so if you are going to be using new components, there will actually be a smaller list.

To give you an idea about how low you can go with specifications, below I will provide a list of the components that I have in my personal use every-day media centre. This is enough capacity to run Blu-ray discs, which is the hardest task your media centre will need to run.

Component	Part Name/Model	Notes
Case	Antec Fusion Remote	
Motherboard	Gigabyte GA-VM900M	Intel 775 pin socket
CPU	Intel Pentium E2200	2.20GHz, dual processor
RAM	4 GB Kingston	2 x 2 GB sticks
Power Supply	Antec Earthwatts 430	430 watts
Audio	High Definition Audio	Built into graphics card
Remote Control	iMon remote	Built into case
Graphics Processor	Gigabyte GV-R577UD-1GD	ATI Radeon HD 5770
Networking	Apower Gigabit Network Card	Realtek 8169 SC chipset
Tuner Cards	Hauppauge Nova TD500	Twin tuner
Hard Drives	150GB Samsung (operating system & data) IDE	300GB Seagate (data) SATA
Operating System	Windows 7 Home Premium	

So, now that you know how low you can go, let's look at each component in more detail.

:: The Case

Cases are arguably the most important part of your media centre. It is the centrepiece of your home entertainment system and will reflect you, your style, and your home.

There are a wide variety of cases on the market, and there is no perfect case. It depends on what you like and what you want.

There are a couple of key elements to think about in deciding which case you want to use:

1. Style / Appearance
2. Space
3. Functionality

Style and Appearance

To me, the look of your media centre case is extremely important. Some people like a clean, elegant-looking case, while others like feature-rich, buttonintensive cases. My very first media centre case was literally a standard midi-tower PC case. It was not attractive, but it worked well.

Overall though, the choice is yours.

Do a Google search for 'media centre case' or 'home theatre pc case' and discover the thousands of different styles out in the market. There is no right or wrong choice.

A word of advice though. If you are like me and you are style-challenged, get some help with basic colour selection. Should you use a silver case or a black one? What colour lights work best in your lounge / theatre room? Should the media centre be seen at all; or should it be the centre piece of your room?

Space

Part of the planning process for your media centre needs to include where you expect to house your beautiful new media centre. Will it be in the TV cabinet? Is it going to be the centre piece of your home entertainment system?

The amount of space you have will narrow down the possible options for the size of your case. This, in turn, will influence the components you will require for the building process.

Cooling and airflow around the case need to be considered. I like to leave at least 50mm on the sides and rear, where possible, to aid with air flow through the case. This will keep the components running cooler, and help them to last longer. More importantly, cooler devices run their fans at a slower speed, meaning less noise.

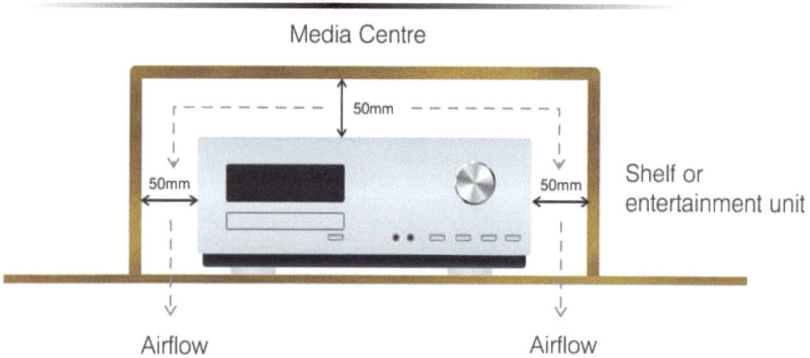

Media Centre

50mm

50mm   50mm   Shelf or
                                          entertainment unit

Airflow   Airflow

Functionality

Each media centre case on the market has its pluses and minuses, so functionality becomes a deciding factor in which case you choose. Do you want a touch screen? In fact, do you want any screen at all? Do you want Fire-wire (a IEEE 1394 connection)? Do you want to add photos from your camera via an SD or CFM card? Do you want any optical drives (Blu-ray)?

I group these functions into two categories:

1. Functional
2. Aesthetic

:: **Functional**

Under functional, you need to think about what kind of connections you will need. Some common connectors are:

USB

IEEE 1394

SD Card

Camera Card

Mini USB

Headphone/Microphone jack

All media centres will have USB connectivity, however this is usually at the back of the media centre, which can be very inconvenient. Do you want your USB at the front (making it ideal for connecting external hard drives)?

Headphone jacks on media centres are typically 3.5mm – if you plan to use the bigger ¼" jack, you may require an adapter.

Optical drives also come under the functionality heading. Optical drives come in three flavours:

CD

DVD

Blu-ray

CDs are obsolete and you will be hard pressed to find them for sale these days, however, both DVD players and Blu-ray players play CDs. A case without provision for an optical drive can be much slimmer – most slim-line cases do not have optical drives. If you are not going to have an optical drive, keep in mind that you will find it more difficult to install your chosen operating system when it comes time to start the software installation. I will cover methods to overcome this in a later chapter.

You should also consider how many hard drives you want to install. I will cover hard drives later as well, but think about how many you may want before you start the building process. There are some very good (and preferable) options to internal hard drive storage which I will discuss later. When it comes to the case, I recommend that you think about one or two drives only.

Many slim-line cases will only have room for one hard-drive, so if you expect or want more, look at a larger / standard-sized case, or a NAS (network attached storage) device.

:: Aesthetics

Aesthetics include features such as:

Fascia finish (ie: metallic or mirror)

Display screen

Lights

Touch screen functionality

Dials / Knobs

As mentioned earlier, the finish of your media centre can greatly influence the look of your lounge or home theatre room. If you are unsure, seek advice from family and friends before making a final decision.

Screen size and functionality is a personal choice. If you would rather see what is playing on your media centre, even when the main TV screen is switched off, then a display screen of some sort is preferable.

Many media centre cases come with a display screen built in, however be aware that some do not. You can install a third party display screen if you so desire – just be sure that you have the space in your chosen case to allow for this. If building for the first time, I would strongly recommend buying a case with a display screen pre-installed.

There are even display screens that have touch functionality, so you can use the media centre navigation without the need to have your main screen on. These touch screens are not cheap, however they do add a big WOW factor to your media centre!

If you like the more minimalistic approach, then there are plenty of cases that do not have any display at all. These are a much cleaner style of case and fit in very well with other home theatre components (a/v receivers, pre amps, etc...).

Key Issues to Consider When Choosing a Case

1. Do you want slim-line or full size?
2. How much space do you have for your media centre?
3. Are you including an optical drive?
4. How many hard drives will you use?
5. What type of display do you want?

Brands to Look For

Antec

OrigenAE

Lian Li

Silverstone

Zalman

MonoAural

:: Motherboard Selection

Motherboards form the basis, or foundation, of any computer and your media centre is no different. The choice of motherboard is based on three key factors:

Form factor (size)

Type of CPU being used

Type and number of expansion slots available

There are some other less critical factors which also should be considered:

Number of SATA data ports

Number of RAM slots

Other onboard features

Form Factor

Motherboards come in 5 standard sizes (also known as form factors) which have been standardised over the years within the computer industry. These sizes, at the time of printing, are:

Form Factor	Size	Expansion Slots
ATX	305 x 244 mm	6
Micro ATX	244 x 244 mm	3
Mini ITX	170 x 170 mm	1
Nano ITX	120 x 120 mm	0
Pico ITX	100 x 72 mm	0

To make things really confusing, there are actually many more different sizes on the market – I have counted at least 36!! However, these are mostly based on the above dimensions, or are used in specific applications like mobile phones, servers, etc...

Pico-ITX

Nano-ITX

Mini-ITX

Micro-ATX

Standard-ATX

One of the great things about building your own media centre is the ability to upgrade it at a later date. So, it is best to stick to standard sizes so that when you do upgrade (and you will!), you can use off-the-shelf items and not be locked in to using expensive proprietary-based components or, even worse, obsolete items requiring a completely new build.

The actual size of the motherboard you choose will be greatly influenced by the type of media centre case you use, however it will boil down to one of two sizes:

Micro ATX   *Mini ITX*

These two sizes utilise the current standard PC CPUs – either Intel or AMD – and have enough expansion slots to ensure that you can add at least one TV tuner – something critical for a media centre.

With the relentless rate of computer development over the last twenty years, Mini ITX boards are fast becoming a media centre favourite because you can use them in smaller cases. This is especially true with the inclusion of high definition on-board graphic processors and high definition on-board audio. These allow you to output a 3D 1080p image with HD audio, using a HDMI cable, without the need for a dedicated Graphics Processor Unit. More on this later...

Type of CPU Being Used

The brand of CPU you use is entirely personal and will be covered in another section, however be aware that you must make sure that the motherboard will take the CPU you plan on using. As already mentioned, there are currently only two brands worth considering:

AMD
Smarter Choice

(intel)

All the motherboard websites have a listing that shows exactly what CPUs can be used. This information is based on their testing, meaning that if it is on their website, and it doesn't work, they will have to supply you with something that does.

21

Number of Expansion Slots

Depending on how you plan to use your media centre, you will need at least one expansion slot for a TV tuner. However, what if you are using extenders? How many tuners will you need? Let's look at a typical scenario:

Dad wants to build a media centre so he can watch and record TV, store movies, CD's and photos. But he also has two teenage kids who have their own bedrooms and TVs, not to mention taste in movies and music.

The two kids each have an Xbox for gaming in their bedrooms so Dad figures it makes sense for these to be used as media extenders too.

In this scenario, there could easily be four TV tuners in use at the same time:

1. Live TV on the media centre
2. Recording a second TV show on the media centre
3. Teenager 1 watching a channel on their extender
4. Teenager 2 watching something different on their extender

In order to meet this highly probable scenario, you will need at least two twin TV tuners installed on your media centre, meaning that you will need at least TWO expansion slots on your motherboard. This immediately narrows your motherboard choice to the Micro ATX form factor.

Generally though, if your media centre is not going to be connected to extenders, then a single twin tuner will be fine.

Other Factors

There are numerous other factors you should consider when choosing your motherboard. Below are three that may influence your final decision.

SATA Ports

How much storage space do you want for your digital media? Will you add it all now, or expand it later when you run out? Will you have an optical drive – a DVD or Blu-ray player?

The number of drives is solely dependent on the number of SATA ports available on your chosen motherboard. The form factor will give you a guide:

Form Factor	SATA Ports
Micro ATX	4
Mini ITX	2

If you plan on adding more internal data storage in the future, then Micro ATX is the better option, however if you plan on using network storage – either a server or a NAS (Network Accessable Storage), then the Mini ITX will be fine.

RAM

How much RAM do you want? The more RAM you add, the faster and smoother your media centre will run. A media centre will run with no problems using 2GB of RAM, meaning you only need one RAM slot. However, you can 'boost' your system with more. Either way, both the Micro ATX and the Mini ITX come with two RAM slots. If you want more than that (and why would you?), then you will need to move to the bigger ATX form factor.

You also need to be aware that the operating system can limit how much RAM you use. This only applies to using Windows.

Windows 32-bit operating systems (including Vista 7 & 8) have a physical limit of 4GB of RAM. You can install more, but these 32-bit operating systems simply won't read it. To overcome this, use the 64-bit versions as they do not have this limitation, and you should be using a 64-bit operating system anyway.

USB Ports

If you plan on using external storage drives – commonly called USB drives – then transfer speeds are an important factor to consider. Currently USB ports come in two modes:

USB 2

USB 3

USB 2 is the current standard, however it is being superseded by USB 3 which offers significantly faster data transfer rates. USB2 is rated at 480Mbps; while USB 3 is rated at 5Gbps. That's a 10 x speed increase – however, in the real world you are more likely to see around 4 x faster file transfers, but this is still a BIG improvement!

Data transfer speed can be important when watching a hi-definition movie from a USB drive. USB 3 will also allow you to stream data from a USB drive while doing other data transfers on the same drive with no perceptible lags, or pauses, in playback.

Also note that USB 3 is backwards compatible with USB 2, so any of your older USB drives will work with a USB 3 port.

What Brand of Motherboard Should I Choose?

There are a wide range of brand names you can choose from when it comes to purchasing a motherboard. Well-known brands such as Intel, ASUS, Gigabyte and AMD all offer quality products that are well-tested and have good return policies should you need this.

Generally, motherboard manufacturers are all quite good, but always – and I mean always – spend the time on due diligence. Check online for what other people are saying about the motherboard you want to use. In Google, use search terms like:

"[motherboard model] problems"

"[motherboard model] faults"

"[motherboard model] reviews"

where [motherboard model] is the brand name and model number of the motherboard you are planning to use (ie: "ASUS 5KP67" or "Gigabyte JH82-KPL").

Key Things to Look For When Choosing a Motherboard

1. What size board fits in your preferred media centre case?
2. What brand of CPU will you use – Intel or AMD?
3. What type of expansion slots will you need?
4. How many expansion slots will you need?
5. How much do you want to spend?

Brands to Look For

ASUS

Intel

Gigabyte

Jetway

:: Central Processing Unit

The Central Processing Unit (CPU for short) is the heart of any computer. It is the part that does all the 'thinking' and 'calculating', enabling us to do all sorts of amazing things – including watching hi-definition movies on our media centre.

Virtually all CPUs are made by one of two companies:

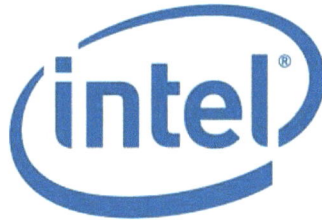

The choice of which brand you use is entirely up to you. For a media centre, there is little to no difference between the two brands. Personally, I use Intel CPUs simply because that is what I have always used.

CPU performance is measured in a couple of different ways. I will explain them here so that you can get an understanding of what the various specifications mean, and so that you can make an informed decision.

CPUs are measured / rated by the following criteria:

> Number of Cores
>
> Speed (in MHz)
>
> Socket type
>
> Cache size and speed

Let's look at these individually, starting with:

Number of Cores

Today's CPUs actually have multiple processors on each chip. Terms like 'Duo' and 'Quad' refer to the number of processors on board. Why is this good? Put simply: they result in reduced processing time.

Multiple processors are able to process multiple tasks at the same time. An analogy for this is a road. A single lane road (single core processor) will only let one car through at a time, whereas a four lane road (quad core processor) can allow four cars through at the same time.

You may also hear a term called 'multi-threading'. This is the action of a processor running multiple tasks at the same time. In effect, this is the ability of the processor to divide a single task into smaller jobs that the all the cores can act simultaneously. This can significantly improve CPU-intensive tasks.

I would also like to point out that a media centre does not need multiple core processors. A dual core processor is ideal, but a media centre will work quite well with a single core processor. My very first media centre used only a single-core Intel Pentium Pro processor. I only upgraded when Blu-ray came onto the scene. Blu-ray is much more CPU-intensive than other media formats, therefore a dual-core processor is the minimum specification required for Blu-ray.

Speed

CPU speed is actually a measurement of frequency, measured in megahertz (MHz). Basically, the larger the number is, the faster the processor, speed is good! I always recommend buying the fastest processor you can afford. Like the number of cores, a media centre does not need the fastest processor on the market, however

It never hurts to have more hertz!

When looking at a processor, anything over 1.2 MHz is fine and will be capable of running / processing Blu-ray movies.

Socket Type

Both CPU manufacturers have different socket types and shapes. It is VERY important that you make sure that your motherboard matches your CPU socket type.

I repeat: **It is VERY important that you make sure that your motherboard matches your CPU socket type.**

Even the same manufacturer has different socket types, and they are constantly developing and evolving their products.

At the time of printing, these are the common socket types for the two manufacturers. However, note that these do change quite rapidly.

Intel	LGA 775	Celeron, Pentium
	LGA 1155	Ivy Bridge
	LGA 1156	i3, i5, i7, Xeon
	LGA 2011	i7

AMD	Socket 939	Athlon, Opteron, Seperon
	Socket 940	Athlon, Opteron
	AM2	Athlon, Opteron2, Phenom
	FM1	A2, A4, A6, E2, Athlon2

The key is to make sure that the motherboard has the same socket type as your processor. If they are not compatible, your system will not work.

The Cache

The cache is an often quoted, and often misunderstood, term in relation to computer performance. Essentially, the cache is a special form of memory that the CPU can use to help it to perform repetitive tasks quickly. It is a special area of memory that is super-fast, and is only accessible by the CPU. RAM (another form of memory) will be discussed later – the main difference between the two is that programs and software have access to RAM – they cannot access the cache.

Even if a CPU does not specify that it has a cache, it still has it. And like computer speed (hertz), the more cache the better. But it is not essential.

If you are on a budget, you can quite easily use a CPU that has a low specification of cache.

Integrated Graphics

The biggest change to processors in recent times has been the advent of the CPU-integrated graphics processor. As the name suggests, current generation processors now have a graphics processor built into the CPU. We touched upon multiple core processors earlier – an integrated graphics processor is one of them!

The advantage of the integrated graphics CPU is that you don't need a dedicated graphics card. This not only saves you some money, it also gives you the opportunity to have a smaller and quieter media centre. It has also opened up the use of highly compact cases.

Key Things to Look For When Choosing a CPU

1. Does the CPU socket type match your motherboard?
2. How many cores does the processor have?
3. What is the speed in MHz? The faster the better.
4. How much cache does the CPU have? The more the merrier.
5. No, really: Does the CPU socket type match your motherboard?

Brands to Look For

Intel

AMD

VIA (for very small pico-sized cases)

:: CPU Coolers

A CPU can generate quite a lot of heat. For this reason, every CPU comes with a cooler – basically a bunch of aluminium fins with a small fan on top to generate airflow and dissipate heat.

For a media centre, these standard coolers are fine and will do the job nicely. A media centre does not over-tax the CPU, so it never gets really hot. However, the cooler is a fan and fans make noise. The holy grail for media centres is one that makes no noise at all.

There is a wide range of CPU coolers on the market that don't use fans. These fall into two fundamental categories:

> Air cooled
>
> Water cooled

Air Cooled

Air coolers are by far the most common, and are the type that come with your CPU. They may or may not come with a fan, depending on the design of the cooler.

If you opt for a fanless air cooler, try to get one with cooling tubes. These tubes help to dissipate the heat from the centre of the cooler faster, making them more efficient.

Pros   Cheap
Small

Cons   Not highly efficient
Can be noisy with fans

Water Cooled

If you are serious about cooling, then the water cooler is the best option. They are much more efficient at cooling – a baby water cooler is far more effective at cooling than the best air cooler. Think about cars – are they air or water cooled? They are water cooled for a good reason!

If you are going to use a water cooler be aware of size. Make sure you are 100% certain that it will fit into your media centre case. Once you have fitted it to a CPU, your local supplier is unlikely to take it back.

Pros   Very efficient
Generally quiet

Cons   Expensive
Size

At the end of the day, an air cooler for your CPU will be fine. I generally use the one that comes with the CPU. Unless you sit very close to the media centre and have no background noise at all, you will not notice any cooler noise.

Key Things to Look For When Choosing a CPU Cooler

1. Air or water cooled?
2. Fan or fanless?

Brands to Look For

Corsair

Coolermaster

Thermaltake

Zalman

Noctua

Deepcool

:: Hard Drives

No component in a media centre is more important than any other, but it is fair to say that hard drives do most of the work. Critically, hard drives are where all your data is stored – so choosing a quality hard drive is VERY important.

There are several reputable brands that you can choose from like:

Seagate

Western Digital

Corsair

Hitachi

Samsung

and others.

So how do you choose which one is right for you? And what makes a good media centre hard drive?

There are some key specifications that you need to look at when deciding on which hard drive is best for you. Let's look at these individually, and discover what they mean and how they relate to our media centre needs. The key specs we will discuss are:

Disc Type

Capacity

Spin Rate

Form Factor

Connection Type

Disc Type

There are two distinct types of hard drive available on the market. They are:

Solid State Drives

Magnetic Disc Drives

The traditional and more well-known hard drive is the magnetic hard disc drive (HDD). These work by reading data off a hard disc which is coated in a magnetic film. This film holds the data which can be read by a movable 'head'. This is the same concept as the old cassette tape – but the difference is the technology used to read the data from the magnetic film. HDDs have been around for a long time and have become so highly developed that you can now buy 3 terabyte drives quite cheaply. We will cover this in detail shortly, but 3 Tb = 3,000,000 Mb, or more than 1 million songs!!

HDDs have the advantage of cost and capacity over solid-state drives, however they are not as fast and are noisier.

Solid State Drives (SSD) are a newer technology that uses integrated circuits to store data. This is the same technology used by RAM chips, which we discuss shortly. This makes SSDs significantly faster than HDDs.

The other major advantage is that they have no moving parts. This makes them more durable (which is why you find them in smart phones and mp3 players) and quieter.

The drawbacks of SSDs are their cost and capacity. SSDs, being a newer technology, are significantly more expensive than their HDD counterparts – although the gap is closing every year. SSDs also store far less data than a HDD – at the moment. I have no doubt that this will change in time.

So which one should you opt for??

In a perfect world I would suggest both, but for different tasks:

SSD – for the operating system. Use the speed and noiselessness to your advantage by using a SSD solely for the operating system. You will only need a small capacity drive (60Gb is plenty).

HDD – for all your data storage. Use the excessive capacity that HDDs have to hold as much data as you can. A 3Tb drive will hold a LOT of HD TV recordings!

Capacity

Size matters, that's all there is to it. When it comes to media centre storage, more is never enough. Once you start using your media centre, you will be surprised how quickly you will fill a 1TB drive.

So, let's talk about capacity and how it is measured. Hard drives are currently measured by the number of gigabytes (GB) or terabytes (TB) that they hold. Here is a chart explaining what I mean:

Capacity	Abbreviation	Comparison
1 Byte	B	8 bits
1 Kilobyte	KB	1,000 bytes
1 Megabyte	MB	1,000 KB
1 Gigabyte	GB	1,000 MB
1 Terabyte	TB	1,000 GB (1,000,000 Mb)
1 Petabyte	PB	1,000 TB
1 Exabyte	EB	1,000 PB

You get the idea. So when you are looking at a drive, you now know that 2 TB is much bigger than 750 GB :)

My recommendation is to get the biggest capacity drive that you can afford – it will last you longer and will help keep your power consumption down because you will have less drives in your media centre.

Spin Rate

Spin rate is exactly what it sounds like. It is a measure of how fast a HDD is spinning. The key here is HDD. SSDs do not have a spin rate as they have no moving parts.

HDDs operate by reading data from the magnetic material that is coated on small, thin hard discs. The head moves over these discs as they are spinning to read and write data. The faster the spin rate, the faster the read/write speed, meaning the faster that content can be delivered to your TV screen.

Having said that, your HD content can only be displayed at a set rate, otherwise everything would be in super fast-forward mode on your TV.

Common spin rates for HDDs are 5,400 rpm and 7,200rpm. There are faster spin rates available, 15,000 rpm for example, however these faster spin rates are very expensive and are designed for corporate servers where multiple users are accessing the drives at the same time.

For a media centre, a 5,400 rpm spin rate is fine. This means that you can utilise older drives if you have them lying around. It is still preferable to use a 7,200 rpm drive, especially if you are installing the operating system on it.

Form Factor

There are two sizes for internal hard drives:

> 3.5"
> 2.5"

The 3.5" drives are the standard size and most HDDs come in this size. Virtually all media centre cases are able to mount a 3.5" drive. There are a few exceptions in the very small cases.

SSDs, however, only come in 2.5" sizing. This is the same as you will find in laptop computers.

Something to keep in mind when you are installing an SSD is that most cases have 3.5" drive bays. This is VERY common. Most SSDs will come with a 3.5" drive bay adaptor, enabling you to fit your drive, but not all do! You need to check before you buy! If necessary, you can purchase a 3.5" to 2.5" drive bay adaptor from your local supplier.

Internal vs External vs NAS

There are three fundamental ways to store your media. All of them use hard drives – the variation is in their location.

An internal drive is one that is located inside the media centre case. All the commentary on hard drives in this book has been oriented towards internal drives.

An external drive is a drive that you connect via a USB cable to the media centre. They are normally used for backing up data or for transferring data to your internal drives. However, you can also use them for permanent storage but this is not recommended because an external drive can be easily knocked or unplugged at the wrong time exposing you to potential data loss. You are also less likely to know the specs of the internals in the external drive and they are not designed to be used for 'always-on' media centre use.

A NAS is a Network Attached Storage device. It is a computer specifically built to store and stream media. That is its sole function. In essence, it is a server for your media centre. Once setup, there is no screen, no keyboard, and no mouse. It is just a series of hard drives with a small computer to control them. You access the NAS over a network – traditionally, a wired home network.

The advantage of a NAS is that you can have more storage than in a normal media centre case. You can also set them up in RAID (Redundant Array of Inexpensive Disks) configuration, which can help with data redundancy in case one of the drives fails.

For first time users, I recommend using internal drives. Once you become a bit more experienced and want to explore other options, then a NAS is worth looking at. Be aware that a NAS does not use a Windows or Linux operating system. They generally use a Unix-based operating system called FreeNAS.

Connectors

There are two basic types of connectors that hard drives use to connect to the motherboard. They are:

IDE

SATA

IDE is the older type and is no longer available, however you may still come across these connectors if you are using older equipment. Most micro-atx motherboards still have a legacy IDE connector on them.

Where possible do not use an IDE drive. They are slower than SATA, more difficult to set up, and they restrict cooling because of the large, wide cable.

SATA is the current standard connector. It is designed as a 'plug and play' type connector. There is only one way for it to be fitted to the motherboard. It also has faster data transfer rates than IDE, and has a much smaller cable, helping airflow inside your media centre.

There are different specifications of SATA. The cables and connectors are all interchangeable, however the transfer speeds are not. You need to have compatible hardware to take advantage of the newer SATA versions and the speeds that they bring.

For example a SATA3 drive (with a transfer rate of 6Mb/s), connected to a SATA2 motherboard (with a transfer speed of 2Mb/s), will only connect at the slower transfer speed. To take advantage of the extra speed of a SATA 3 drive, you will need to connect it to a SATA3 capable motherboard.

Like spin rates, for a media centre, the transfer speed is not critical. Even an IDE connection will work. But if the drive is designed to house your operating system, then you should at the very least use a SATA connection.

Key Things to Look For When Choosing a HDD

1. How much storage space can you afford? More is never enough

2. SSD, HDD or both? SSD = operating system; HDD = data storage

3. What generation of SATA is it? Make sure your motherboard is capable

4. How many drives do you expect to connect?

Brands to Look For

Western Digital

Seagate

OCZ

Kingston

:: Power Supplies

Every machine needs a source of power, be it a bike, a car, or a computer. Choosing the right power supply in the first place, can make a world of difference to your media centre. An underpowered media centre will run intermittently, crash regularly, and in some cases, not even start.

Power supplies (also known as PSUs) are rated by Watts – the amount of power a PSU can supply at peak demand. The complexity of your media centre will determine the minimum rating for your power supply.

Component Consumption

Every component of your media centre will consume power when it is turned on. This includes your CPU, RAM, Motherboard, TV tuners, optical drives, hard drives, and anything else you have attached. Knowing the components that you are going to use to build your media centre allows you to determine the minimum size of the power supply you will need.

Rather than giving you a list of how much power each item consumes (which will be out of date anyway), I recommend that you visit the following websites to determine what size PSU you will need:

http://www.thermaltake.outervision.com/Power

However, I suspect that some of you like to have an idea of what is actually happening, so here is a list anyway. What follows is a general (and I can't stress that enough) guide to what components actually consume.

The ranges given are for idle power consumption all the way up to maximum power consumption. When you are calculating power supply demands, you ALWAYS use the maximum power consumption figures.

CPUs	Intel	35 → 105 watts
	AMD	90 → 160 watts
GPUs	Nvidia	100 → 190 watts
	ATI Radeon	30 → 140 watts

Motherboards	30 ⟶ 90 watts
Hard Drives (each)	10 ⟶ 20 watts
Optical Drives	5 ⟶ 20 watts
RAM	2 ⟶ 5 watts
TV Tuner	30 ⟶ 75 watts

These are rough guides only, based on maximum loadings. Generally your system will not consume this amount of power because it will not be running at full load. Even running a 3D Blu-ray disc will not max out your media centre.

If you plan to use your media centre for gaming as well, then you will want to go for the larger PSUs. Graphics cards are the biggest single consumer of power – which is why the higher-end cards require a direct PSU connection.

I always recommend going to the next size up for your PSU from what you think you will need. Better to be safe than sorry.

Connectors

Also, be aware that not all PSUs come with the same connectors. There are several types of connectors you will need, depending on the components you plan to use. Some of the common connectors currently in use are:

Motherboard 20+4 ATX connector

4 pin ATX connector

8 pin EPS connector

Peripherals
4 pin molex connector

SATA power connector

PCI
6 pin PCI Express connector

8 pin PCI Express connector

The PCI connectors are only used by higher-end dedicated graphics cards. As a rule of thumb, any PSU over 500W will have at least one 6 pin PCI Express power connector and an 8 pin EPS connector.

Efficiency

Power supplies now come with an optional '80 Plus' rating. This rating is a good guide to quality. The rating stipulates that the PSU will supply at least 80% of its maximum rating at peak load. Basically it means that the PSU does not 'waste' too much energy.

There are various levels of 80 Plus – bronze, silver, gold and platinum. These are summarised below for reference. Note that there are two charts – one for 110v power sources and the other for 230v. Essentially a 230v power source is more efficient than the equivalent 110v power source, so the charts reflect this difference.

80 PLUS Test Type	115V Internal Non-Redundant				230V Internal Redundant			
Fraction of Rated Load	10%	20%	50%	100%	10%	20%	50%	100%
80 PLUS		80%	80%	80%				
80 PLUS Bronze		82%	85%	82%		81%	85%	81%
80 PLUS Silver		85%	88%	85%		85%	89%	85%
80 PLUS Gold		87%	90%	87%		88%	92%	88%
80 PLUS Platinum		90%	92%	89%		90%	94%	91%
80 PLUS Titanium					90%	94%	96%	91%

Quality

Finally, a word on quality. It is important to spend a little extra money on a quality known brand of PSU for your media centre. Cheaper brands do not necessarily give out the watts that they claim, they also deteriorate faster, are a lot more prone to complete failure, and are also noisier. The last thing you want to be doing is changing your power supply in six months time.

Key Things to Look For When Choosing a PSU

1. What is your minimum watt rating to run your media centre?

2. Does your PSU have an '80 Plus' rating?

3. Do you have all the connectors you need for your system?

Brands to Look For

Corsair

Antec

Thermaltake

Coolermaster

Zalman

:: Graphics Cards

Now we turn to a controversial topic – graphics cards. In the past, a graphics card was essential for your media centre. Without it, there simply was not enough grunt to be able to play full high-definition media.

In recent years, with the advent of the integrated graphics CPUs by Intel and AMD, you no longer need a separate graphics card.

As long as you have a current motherboard which has a chipset to take advantage of HD-integrated graphics, your media centre will be more than capable of playing

3D 1080p Blu-ray movies with no audio loss through a HDMI cable.

So, if you don't need a graphics card, should you still get one? And if so, what are the factors to consider? The answer to this is yes, if:

1. You plan to do other things with your media centre. Specifically, gaming or any form of 3D rendering
2. You are building a media centre from older components that do not have integrated HD graphics capabilities

For most people these days the answer is no. Therefore, you can skip through to the next section :)

When it comes to graphics cards, there are a couple of key factors that you need to consider:

1. Chipset
2. Size of the card
3. Memory
4. Noise levels

Chipset

Graphics cards come with one of two chipsets:

The chipset is the actual processor that does all the work. Both Nvidia and ATI Radeon have been in the game a long time and both offer features and benefits over each other, and like the CPU brands (Intel and AMD), they are constantly trying to outdo each other. Sometimes, ATI Radeon will be the better chipset, sometimes Nvidia.

At the time of writing this book, ATI Radeon are my recommendation, however this will change, so always conduct your due diligence and check online forums for what users are saying about the two chipsets when you are ready to buy.

Size of the Card

Modern graphics cards are designed primarily for gamers. This means that they are designed to connect multiple monitors (screens) at the same time to allow for a wider field of vision. Most cards these days will actually support three screens running simultaneously. As a media centre user you don't need this functionality.

The trade-off for having multiple monitors is that you need multiple ports to run these monitors. And given that the card height is a standard height, the only way to allow for these extra ports is by making the card wider.

Wider cards will prevent you from using some of the internal expansion slots on the motherboard. If you are going to run several TV tuner cards, this may be an issue for you.

An older card with a small (or no) fan may be your best option. The minimum spec GPU to run Blu-ray is either:

> Nvidia 7 series
>
> ATI Radeon X1600 series
>
> Intel G33

As I said these are the minimum specs – ideally you would like something a little better. My personal recommendations are:

> Nvidia 8 series
>
> ATI Radeon HD2400 series
>
> Intel G45

or higher.

Memory

One of the key advantages of using a dedicated graphics card is that it takes the load off the CPU and frees up all-important RAM for system use.

This is because the GPU has its own processor specifically designed for dealing with the complex rendering calculations that would normally be handled by the CPU. And all of this calculating requires memory - RAM. So, the more on-board memory that a GPU has, the better. Currently, on-board RAM is measured in gigabytes. Any GPU with 1GB or more will easily handle any media centre duties.

There are also different types of on-board RAM. Don't let the marketing jargon confuse you: the type of RAM is not really important, DDR3, GDDR5 – it just doesn't matter. Obviously, newer types of RAM will be faster, but for our purposes, it is irrelevant.

:: *Noise Levels*

Noise is a major factor to consider for any media centre. The last thing you want to hear during a riveting soliloquy is your GPU fan humming away in the background.

Most graphics cards have fans to cool the processors and other components. The more powerful the GPU, the bigger the fan and the noisier it will be, especially under load.

Thankfully there are a number of middle-to-low-end GPUs that are fan-less. If you are going to use a GPU, then these are the cards to go for.

Key Things to Look For When Choosing a GPU

1. Do you really need one?
2. How noisy will it be? Can you go fan-less?
3. How wide is the card? Will it prevent you from using other expansion slots on your motherboard?
4. Does it meet minimum Blu-ray specifications?

Brands to Look For

ASUS

ATI Radeon

HIS

Gigabyte

:: TV Tuners

The bit that makes your media centre a real media centre is the TV Tuner. This small piece of hardware enables you to watch live TV. Depending on where you live, you will get your TV via analogue or digital frequency, satellite or cable.

I will not be dealing with subscription TV (cable TV) in this book as it is quite an extensive and fiddly process. There are resources online that can help you build the specific hardware required to read the decoder card required to watch subscription TV.

The reason why Cable TV is difficult has to do with the encryption used. Foxtel, HBO, and others, encrypt their TV signals to prevent anybody from simply watching their shows – this is why you need a set-top box – it does the encryption decoding so you can watch their shows. So, to watch cable TV through your media requires a method of decoding the encryption – something that the cable TV stations do not encourage.

When selecting a TV tuner, you need to answer three essential questions:

1.   What type of TV signal are you going to receive?

2.   Do you want an internal or external tuner?

3.   Do you want a single or dual tuner?

Once you answer these questions, you are then ready to decide which model/brand of card you want.

TV Signal Type

There are three TV signal types that you are likely to come across:

1.   Analogue (either PAL, NTSC or SECAM)

2.   Digital (DVB-T, ATSC or ISDB)

3.   Satellite (DVB-S or QAM)

To see what each of the abbreviations means, please check the glossary at the back of the book.

Analogue TV signals are being phased out across most of the globe, particularity in more developed countries. In Australia, analogue TV signals will be completely switched off in 2013. There are still some community TV stations that broadcast in analogue, however even they are now switching to digital broadcasting.

That leaves digital or satellite signals. The most common type of TV signal in Australia is DVB-T, or an over-the-air digital TV signal. This means that, in order to watch, record, and do all the other cool things you can with a media centre, you will need to install a DVB-T tuner.

If you receive your digital TV signal via satellite – something a lot of rural people do – then you will need a DVB-S tuner card.

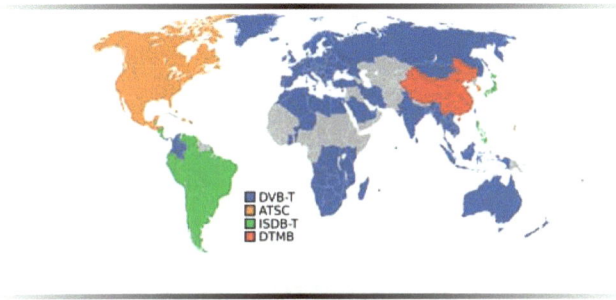

Digital TV formats around the world

Do not get these mixed up! If you get the wrong card, you will not be able to decode the digital TV signal – this will mean no TV.

If you use a cable TV service, like Foxtel, Austel, etc..., then you will need a QAM tuner to decode the TV signal. Please note that a QAM tuner will not decrypt an encrypted TV signal. This means that you will still need your provider's set-top box to decrypt the signal BEFORE feeding it into your media centre.

Internal or External

There are two fundamental types of TV tuners: PCI (internal) or USB (external). Each has their advantages and disadvantages, but ultimately, it will come down to which you prefer.

If you are building a dedicated media centre, then I would recommend the internal, or PCI, TV tuner. These tuners keep all the circuitry and components inside the media centre, making for a much tidier unit. Essentially, all you do is plug the aerial into the back of your media centre and you are set to go.

External TV tuners plug into a spare USB port in your computer. This provides much more flexibility because you can remove the tuner very easily if you need to. Ideal applications for USB tuners are laptops, multi-use machines, and very small media centres where there is no room for a PCI tuner.

The main issue I have with external tuners is that they are a lot easier to damage than an internal PCI tuner.

At the end of the day, both tuners are, in reality, USB tuners. Internal PCI tuners are actually USB tuners mounted on a PCI board which uses the PCI bus to transmit the decoded information to the graphical output (normally your HDMI cable).

Single, Double or Hybrid Tuner

A double tuner will double your TV viewing pleasure. It enables you to watch and record TV at the same time or, if you have an extender, watch two TV signals at the same time. So why would you buy a single tuner? The only reason I can think of is money.

There are a range of twin (double) tuners on the market. The most noticeable difference between them is the number of aerial inputs. Some cards have two inputs which is how they get the two TV signals. The disadvantage of this is that you need – you guessed it – two cables. This means introducing a TV splitter to split the signal from your aerial. This introduces some signal loss which is not ideal.

Other twin tuners have one aerial input and split the TV signal internally. These are my preferred tuners for two reasons:

1.   You only need one aerial cable
2.   They tend to have on-board decoders reducing the load on the CPU

The third choice of tuner is the hybrid. A hybrid tuner combines digital and analogue on the one card. Why you might ask? Well the analogue TV tuner also picks up FM radio. With a hybrid tuner, you can then use digital TV and the FM radio function inside your media centre, meaning you can listen to your favourite local radio station - something that is not always possible using internet radio.

You can even get a TV tuner that is a hybrid, twin tuner: That is 1 x analogue tuner and 2 x digital TV tuners – awesome! (it's the Hauppauge HVR2200, if you are interested).

Signal Quality

Media centres are far more unpredictable when it comes to signal quality. Even though you may get a TV signal on your normal flat screen TV, you are not guaranteed to get a TV signal on your media centre.

There is no obvious reason for this, other than that the TV tuner cards are in an environment that has a lot more electrical interference than your standard TV tuner – a computer. As a result, the cards require a stronger signal to reduce the risk of signal interference.

Also note that a twin tuner will be more susceptible to low signal quality because it needs to split the signal that it receives. A single TV tuner does not have this problem.

If you are having TV signal problems, you should invest in a TV signal amplifier. There are two types on the market:

1. Wall amplifier
2. Masthead amplifier

A wall amplifier is one that you plug into a powerpoint in the wall. You then plug an aerial into the input which boosts the signal strength output.

A masthead amplifier does the same thing, but from the antenna itself. A masthead amplifier is the better option because it boosts the best signal it can get. However, it is also more expensive, as you will need a professional to install it for you.

At the end of the day, an amplifier can only boost the signal strength, not the signal quality.

My suggestion is to get a professional in to check out your antenna and cabling. They will be able to advise if you are getting sufficient signal quality (and strength), and what your options are to improve it, if necessary.

Key Things to Look For When Choosing a TV Tuner

1. What type of TV signal do you receive? Digital or Satellite?

2.   Internal or external? PCI or USB?

3.   Do you want a single, double, or hybrid tuner?

Brands to Look For

Hauppauge

AVerMedia

Leadtek

Compro

Kworld

DViCo

:: Random Access Memory

RAM, as it is known, is extra fast storage space that programs can use to store information while they are processing data or waiting to perform other tasks. RAM is different from cache – which we talked about in the chapter on CPUs – in that it is accessible by all programs, including the operating system. Cache is only available to the processor.

Having a sufficient amount of RAM is critical to smooth playback on your media centre. This is because if you do not have enough RAM, the computer software will start using the hard drive to supplement the physical RAM. It does this by creating a special area called the 'pagefile' which software uses just like RAM, only far slower.

This process is called 'disk caching'. Disk caching makes the hard drive work very, very hard – at 100% capacity – and this limits what your hard drive can do. The upshot of all this is that, when you are disk caching, your media will not stream smoothly. You will get stuttery video and audio, long pauses while another process takes over the hard drive, and generally poor performance.

So how much RAM is enough? Some people will tell you that you can never have enough RAM. For a media centre this is not true. Although more is better, you can safely use a minimum of 2GB (a single 2GB stick of RAM). I have had media centres run on 1GB. It works, but it won't handle Blu-ray.

Basically, 2GB is your minimum.

I have built systems with 16GB of RAM, because that's what the client wanted, however there was no noticeable difference in media playback over a system with 4GB. Nevertheless, the operating system did load VERY quickly, something we'll discuss later on.

Memory Types

As technology develops and evolves, new formats of RAM appear. DDR3 RAM is current at the time of writing, but this will change. The key with RAM is to make sure that the format of RAM you buy matches the requirements of your motherboard. Let's look at a RAM descriptor from Amazon:

> G.SKILL 8GB (2 x 4GB) Ripjaws X Series DDR3 1600MHz 240-Pin PC3-12800 Desktop Memory F3-12800CL9D-8GBXL

Quite a mouthful!

There are three things to take note of:

1. Format
2. Speed
3. Quantity

Format

DDR3 – this is the format of the RAM chip itself. This dictates what type of slot the RAM must fit into. Obviously, you want to make sure that your motherboard has a DDR3 slot for the DDR3 RAM to fit into.

Other, older formats include DDR2 and DDR RAM. On really old motherboards, you may even come across SD RAM. My advice is that, unless you already have sufficient RAM for your older motherboard, you are better off getting new hardware. Yes it costs more, but it will last longer and perform better.

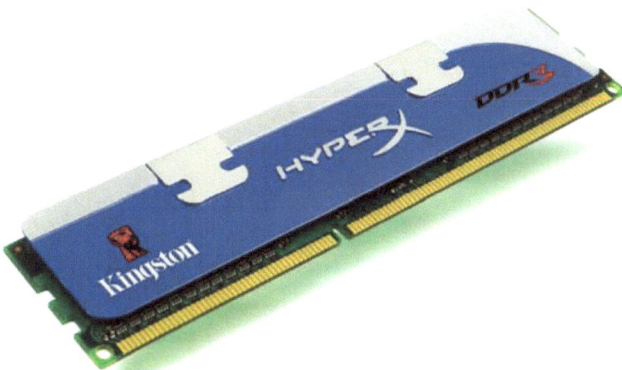

DDR3 Ram Stick

Speed

1600MHz – this is the speed of the RAM, the frequency at which it processes data. Most motherboards will processes several different speeds of RAM. However, if your motherboard does not support that particular speed, you may experience intermittent problems which will not appear to be related, or your media centre may not get through the POST process (explained later – it's the self-test the motherboard does before the operating system is loaded), and therefore will not boot.

At best, faster speed RAM chips will only be accessed at the speed the motherboard is rated at – ie: a 1333MHz motherboard will access 1600MHz RAM at 1333 MHz.

Make sure the speed of your RAM is compatible with your chosen motherboard.

Quantity

2 x 4GB – this indicates that the total memory advertised (8GB) is actually 2 sticks of 4GB of RAM. Make sure you have enough slots available for the number of sticks of RAM you are buying. Nano ITX boards often only have 1 RAM slot available, so two sticks would be a waste of money.

Having two sticks of RAM does gives you the opportunity to take advantage of Dual Channel RAM should your motherboard support it. This is not important for media centres.

Dual Channel RAM essentially doubles the RAM bandwidth from 64bit to 128bit which will give you an increase in overall system performance. This is at the expense of capacity – 2 x 4GB RAM in Dual Channel mode will give you 4GB of RAM, rather than the 8GB you get in Single Channel mode.

Key Things to Look For When Choosing RAM

1. What format of RAM does my motherboard need?
2. What speed RAM do I need? What speed is my motherboard rated at?
3. How much RAM do I want/need?

Brands to Look For

Kingston

Corsair

G.Skill

Patriot

OCZ

:: Remote Controls

A commonly neglected part of any home theatre system is the all-important remote control. There is a wide range of remote controls available on the market, so it is important to make sure you choose one that will suit you and your system.

So which remote should you choose? Let's look at the

key elements:

1.	Communication Methods
2.	Functionality
3.	Extras

These are very broad topics that I will cover individually. Some features and communication methods can add significant cost to your remote, so as always, be informed before you make a final decision (but then, that is why you are reading this book!)

Communication Methods

A remote needs to communicate commands to your media centre that the media centre recognises so it can perform the task you ask of it. In the old days, I remember TV and VCR (remember those??) remotes that were physically connected to the device with a cable. These days we'd call it tethering – but back then it was called 'advanced technology'!

There are four basic methods a remote can use to communicate and connect with your media centre:

1.	Infra-red (IR)
2.	Radio frequency (RF)
3.	Wi-fi
4.	Bluetooth

Each has its own advantages and disadvantages, so let's look at each one:

:: Infrared

Infra-red (IR for short) uses a low frequency light which we can't see. As the name suggests, it is a frequency of light that is below red in the spectrum. This has the advantage of using less power than the other three methods, making the batteries last longer.

IR is also very common. There are quite a few media centre cases that come with IR receivers built-in, making IR remotes an immediate choice for users. IR is also highly developed and follows international standards, giving manufacturers (and therefore, consumers) greater ease and flexibility in developing remotes for multiple purposes and across multiple devices – something we'll talk about shortly.

You will also find that media centres take IR commands as a default. The default protocol for media centre remotes is called IR6 – basically infra-red is the media centre's native command input (other than keyboard and mouse).

There are many IR remotes that come preconfigured with commands for a wide range of TVs, amplifiers, and receivers, making it easy to integrate a single remote into your media centre setup.

The down side of IR is that it consists of light. Anything that blocks the passage of the light will interrupt the IR commands being sent to the media centre. Walls, books, and even coffee cups, can prevent an IR signal from reaching it intended destination. This is known as line of sight and is the main drawback of IR remotes.

Be aware, too, that many IR remotes do not come with an IR receiver – so you may need to purchase one separately.

:: Radio Frequency

The problems associated with IR, is where Radio Frequency (RF) has its greatest strengths. Because radio frequencies have the ability to bend around corners and pass through objects, you can use an RF remote from anywhere.

For example, you can control your media centre in the lounge from the kitchen because you don't need a line of sight for the command to reach the media centre.

An RF remote uses an RF receiver that converts the RF signal into an IR command that is transmitted to the media centre. You can also convert the RF signal to RS232 commands, but that is less common and far more complex to achieve, putting it outside of the scope of this book.

The downside is that you have to convert the RF command to an IR command. This adds cost and complexity to the overall remote control package. Often, there is special programming required in order to teach the remote new commands – in many cases, you will need to pay for someone to do this for you.

:: Wi-fi

Wi-fi uses your media centre's network connection to receive commands from a wi-fi remote. This means you can set up your smart phone or tablet to be a media centre remote – how cool is that! There is a range of iPhone and android apps that will turn your phone/tablet into a media centre remote – something that will impress your friends.

And like RF, wi-fi does not rely on line of sight to transmit commands to the media centre. Also, as long as you have a wi-fi signal from your home network, you can control the media centre – even from a completely different room in your house. There are even a few programs that will allow you to control your media centre over the internet! But I do not recommend this, as it creates a potential security risk for your home network, plus there is little advantage to turning on your media centre when you are not there.

The downside to wi-fi is that you need a wi-fi network setup in your house. This can be a wi-fi router (such as those on wi-fi modems), or a wi-fi card in your media centre.

I STRONGLY SUGGEST YOU DO NOT INSTALL A WI-FI CARD IN YOUR MEDIA CENTRE.

I will say that again in case you missed it:

I STRONGLY SUGGEST YOU DO NOT INSTALL A WI-FI CARD IN YOUR MEDIA CENTRE.

I am not saying you can't (I have done it a few times for clients that insisted), but it is not recommended.

If you are uncomfortable with setting a wi-fi network, it is best not to use this option.

:: Bluetooth

This is the least common of the communication methods because it is relatively expensive, there are few devices available on the market, and you need a Bluetooth receiver on your media centre, which is not common.

There are other issues with Bluetooth as well:

1. Bluetooth drains batteries a lot faster than other methods
2. There is a delay of several seconds when Bluetooth switches on. A lot of Bluetooth devices turn themselves off after a period of inactivity to conserve battery power

Like RF and wi-fi, you don't need a line of sight to control the media centre.

Basically, your choice will come down to either IR or RF, depending on your needs, and what else you expect to control with your new remote. Which leads us to:

Functionality

What do you expect your remote to actually control? If you are planning a typical media centre setup, you will most likely have:

D. A media centre
E. A flat screen TV or projector
F. An AV receiver

Your media centre remote should be able to control all of these items, including functions like:

1. Power on and off all devices
2. Volume control of TV or AV receiver
3. Media centre commands

But you may also want to control more. What about any automated devices around the house? What about lighting systems? Heating and cooling systems? Will you want to control more than one type of TV or receiver?

The more you want to control, the more likely you are to want to run macros. A macro is a sequence of commands that are activated at the press of a button. An example of a macro is if you push a button called "Watch TV" the following commands are issued in the following order:

1. Turn on AV receiver

2.   Turn on TV
3.   Turn on Media Centre
4.   Set TV to HDMI input 3
5.   Set AV Receiver to HDMI input 4
6.   Set AV Receiver to HDMI output 2

So, rather than pressing 6 buttons, you just press one.

Extras

The remote will become the focal point of your media centre system because it is the most used piece of equipment. So, it makes sense to think about how you want it to look. What colour will go with your décor? Should it be something that fits in one hand, or would you prefer something that you can rest on your lap?

You will also want to consider the remote control buttons. Do you want hard buttons, or a touch screen? If you want a touch screen, does it need to be in colour?

Do you want to program the remote or would you like someone else to do it for you? Some of the popular remotes enable you to set up the programming yourself using software that you can install on your media centre or another computer. These can be complex at times, but they usually come with online support to help you though the process.

Do you want the remote to have learning capability? Learning functions enable your remote to capture an IR command that it does not recognise – say an air-conditioning system – and then assign that command to a button. This means that you can issue the command at the press of a button or include it in a macro.

Overall, I suggest you spend some time (and money) on getting the right remote for you. A cheap remote will not only break down reasonably quickly, be difficult to use, and feel flimsy, but it will detract from the experience of owning your own media centre.

Key Things to Look For When Choosing a Remote Control

1. Do you want IR or RF control?
2. Will it control all the devices you want it to?
3. Does the appearance and style of the remote suit your home and media centre system?
4. Do you need a separate IR or RF receiver?

Brands to Look For

Logitech Harmony
RTI
Crestron

:: Networking

To get the best out of your media centre you will want to connect it to a network, or the internet. You don't need to, but it will give you the opportunity to listen to internet radio, download updates and other media, plus give you the ability to play around with plug-ins.

We'll talk about plug-ins later, but it is important to discuss networking and connectivity options.

You have two basic options when it comes to connecting to the internet or your home network:

1. Ethernet
2. Wi-fi

Let's discuss the pros and cons of each.

Ethernet

Ethernet is the standard network cable that you plug into your modem or router to give you direct physical access to a network. This is secure, fast, and cheap to set up. You use either a Cat5 or Cat6 specification cable to make the connection.

There are three speeds that you will come across, although the first is rare as it is quite old:

10 Mbit

100 Mbit

1 Gbit

A megabit is different to a megabyte. There are 8 bits in a byte, so a 10Mbit connection will enable you to transfer a maximum of 1.25 megabytes per second, 100Mbit will allow 12.5 megabytes per second, and 1Gbit will allow a maximum of 125 megabytes per second.

10 Mbit is obsolete these days, however network devices are capable of communicating at this speed, if required.

The two common speeds you will find are 100Mb and 1Gb (which is 1,000Mb). Both of these speeds are more than adequate to stream high-definition media over an internal network. If you are running extenders, both will work, however I would recommend that you use Gigabit cabling and equipment where possible.

It is also worth noting that a network's speed is determined by the slowest component, just like a relay team's speed is determined by the slowest runner. If you have older 100Mb devices, but use 1Gb cabling, you will only be able to achieve a maximum speed of 100Mbit.

These days, all motherboards come with 1Gbit ethernet connections, so there is no need to add any special hardware to your media centre. Everything you need is already there!

Wi-fi

Do not use wi-fi for media centres - plain and simple.

Why? Well wi-fi is affected by interference far more than ethernet. It is also subject to a far higher loss ratio than ethernet.

But more than that, wi-fi signals are significantly affected by flat screen TVs – plasmas, in particular. Think about where a media centre will most likely be placed. Usually, it is underneath a flat screen TV, possibly in an entertainment system shelf. If you have a wi-fi card in your media centre, this places the antenna behind the TV screen, where the most interference is found.

Wi-fi is not great for streaming high-definition media. Yes, it can be done, but not reliably, unless your media centre is very close to your wi-fi router. But, if it's that close, why not use a cable?

In my experience, wi-fi causes too many problems when used with a media centre. Take my advice and DON'T DO IT.

Home Networks

A quick word on home networks. A home network can be of great use to your media centre experience. If you set up a home server, you can store all your media safely on a second device and then stream that media to your media centre. By utilising plug-ins and the like, you can have daily backups of all your media, including family photos, videos, and music.

Although beyond the scope of this book, setting up a home network is not too difficult, especially if you have already built your own media centre.

The ultimate setup is to have a home server that stores all your media, which is then accessed by the media centre, any extenders, and all your smart devices (like laptops, phones, tablets etc...). The server stores all the digital media and 'serves' out the data as required. The advantage of this is that the media centre is freed from the task of dishing out media. Its resources are now focused on playing content.

:: Summary

The components you choose to make your media centre will have a large part to play in your overall experience. You don't need the best, or the latest, components to make it work, but you should spend a few extra dollars on some key parts. As a guide, I recommend the following:

Case	Personal choice
Motherboard	Get the most up to date you can. Must be compatible with processor
Processor	Get the most up to date you can. Must be compatible with motherboard
HDD	Size matters, but so does quality. Stick with a well-known brand
Remote	Simple systems should use IR. If you can afford it, RF is great!
RAM	The more the merrier
GPU	If you don't use the on-board GPU, get something as quiet as possible
TV Tuner	Reliability is the key. Make sure the format suits your input signal (terrestrial, cable or satellite)
PSU	Get a well-known brand with '80 Plus' certification

To give you some idea, my personal media centre (which is also one of my test beds) has the following specs:

> Motherboard: Gigabyte GA-VM900M
>
> CPU: Intel E2200 – 2.2 MHz, dual core processor
>
> RAM: 4Gb
>
> GPU: ATI Radeon HD5700 (no in-built GPU on the motherboard)
>
> Audio: Built into GPU
>
> OS: Windows 7 and 8 64 bit
>
> Case: Antec Fusion (has built-in IR receiver)
>
> Remote: Logitec Harmony 525 (IR remote)

Certainly not high end, but it works – and works well.

When you put all of these things together, you end up with a personal computer. It's what we do with it that will make it a true media centre.

Part 2

:: The Build

For many people, building a media centre, or computer, seems like a daunting task, but it isn't. In fact, modern computers are quite easy to build. They are designed to be as straightforward and user-friendly to build as they are to use.

In Part 2, we look at the build process and actually go through it step-by-step. In Part 1, we discussed what components you need, and gave you some tips and tricks on working out the best parts for you. Now, we will put those components together and end up with a working system which we can then configure into a full blown media centre!

:: Preparation Area

Before we start building a media centre, we need an area that is suitable. It doesn't have to be a sterile, electrostatically neutral room. But it should be:

Dust-free – as far as is reasonably possible
Free of clutter
Well-lit
Have plenty of space

Dust-Free

When I say dust-free, we are not talking about a biological isolation room. However, we do want to minimise the amount of dust in the room. This means:

1. A non-carpeted room is preferred
2. You should have the windows closed to prevent drafts
3. You should not be smoking
4. Animals should be kept out of the room

Dust can cause problems. It is rare, but dust can get in-between a CPU and the motherboard, preventing contact on the pins, rendering the motherboard/CPU useless. And it will take you a long time to figure this out, trust me.

Free of Clutter / Plenty of Space

Building a media centre is quite straightforward. However, there are several parts that will be needed, all which come in their own packaging. You will be using a number of small screws to hold everything together – and these are very easy to lose.

A clear area – for example, a clean desk or table – is ideal. Don't have loose papers lying around. If you want to be really organised, get a few jar lids to hold the loose screws.

It is also good to have a separate area to put the component packaging when you have finished with it. There will be quite a lot of waste cardboard and plastic. Virtually all of it will be recyclable – please do so, if you can. Flatten all the cardboard and separate the plastics, and then place it into your recycling bin.

Having said that, I do recommend keeping the motherboard box and the case box. You can use the motherboard box to store all the little manuals and driver CDs that came with your components. The case box becomes a terrific way to transport your media centre should you ever have to do so. It fits the case perfectly and consists of shock absorbing high-density foam.

Well-Lit

When building your media centre, you will need a lot of light. Shadows make it hard to find where components need to be plugged in. This is especially true when connecting cables to the motherboard.

A well-lit room will make it easier to fit and install cables. It is also much easier to find little screws and things that fall out of your hands. And that will happen ...

Natural sunlight is best, however, in reality, any strong lighting from the ceiling will do. Down lights are perfect, but any ceiling light will suffice. If you can't get strong light from your ceiling, you will need a lamp and/or torch. Make sure that you lamp has a bright globe in it – 100w or equivalent is ideal.

If you use a torch, it should be small, but powerful – the newer-style LED keyring torches are perfect.

:: Tools

Now that you have a good working area, you will need a few tools. Not all of these are mandatory, but they will be of use at some stage during the build.

Make sure you have the following – you will not be able to build your media centre without them:

Phillips Head screw-driver

Pen knife

There are some other tools that are not essential, but are useful:

1. Small torch

2. Needle nose pliers

3. Electric screwdriver

4. Diagonal cutters

5. Cable ties

6. Jewellery screwdriver set

7. Small containers or unused jar lids

8. Flat screwdriver

Having these around will make life that little bit easier, especially when you drop a screw into that hard to get to place - and it will happen!

:: The Build

We will break the build process into 5 stages. You should do all of the stages in sequence. I would recommend that if it is your first time building a computer, to allow 3 hours, so that you can take your time and get each step right.

If you have built a computer before, then you can gloss over these instructions, or just head straight to Part 3 – installing the software.

For the rest of us, these are the stages:

1. Motherboard (including CPU and RAM)
2. Case preparation (including drives)
3. Cables
4. PCI cards
5. First boot

So let's get started!

Motherboard

Items required:

>Motherboard
>CPU
>RAM
>Heatsink (if not using the one that comes with the CPU)

Open the motherboard box and pull out all the bits. You will need most of them, so keep them to one side.

1. Take motherboard from the plastic bag and place onto foam/cardboard base that came with the box

2. Open the CPU box and unpack the CPU.

3. On the motherboard, take off the protective cover from the CPU socket.

4. Lift the CPU mounting bracket up by pushing down on the small lever and pushing to one side. The bracket will rise by itself.

5. Place the CPU gently on to the socket. DO NOT FORCE THE CPU.

    1. The CPU will only fit one way. Look for the indentations on one side of the CPU and align with the CPU socket.

    2. When you place the CPU on the socket, rest on one side of the socket, and then gently lower the CPU into place.

6. Take the CPU fan out of the CPU box.

7. Place the fan over the CPU as per the instructions. Check the user manual of the motherboard/CPU or CPU Cooler for more specific details. You will need to align the four clips of the fan with the holes on the motherboard. The fan clips are like the feet of the fan.

8. Gently press the feet into the holes on the motherboard until they click into place.

1. You will know when you have all four feet in place by trying to rock the CPU fan. If it moves they are not in yet.

2. Once in place rotate the top of the feet to lock the feet in place.

MEDIA CENTRES MADE EASY

3. If you need to have another try, use a flat
    head screwdriver to undo the feet locking
    mechanism (rotate clockwise). You can then
    lift the clip and try again.

9. Plug the CPU fan power plug into the appropriate
   pins on the motherboard.

1. The power pins will be located in different
   places, depending on which motherboard you
   have. Refer to the motherboard user manual for
   specific information.

2. If you are using a different CPU fan, please
   refer to the fan installation guide. But the basic
   process is the same :)

Now we do the RAM:

10. Open the RAM pack and remove the RAM.

11. Place the RAM into the RAM slots, as shown. The RAM chip will only fit in one way.

12. Once you are happy that the RAM is in the right way, press down firmly on the ends until you hear a satisfying 'snap' from the clips at each end.

At this stage, the motherboard can be put back into the plastic bag, or put aside, while we carry out the next step – preparing the case.

The Case

Items required:

> Case
>
> Power supply
>
> Motherboard backing plate
>
> Completed motherboard from Stage 1
>
> HDD/SSD/DVD
>
> Small pliers/tweezers
>
> Phillips Head screwdriver

Open the box holding your case, and remove the case. It is recommended to keep the foam packaging and the box for a period of time, because it is very handy if you need to transport the completed media centre. Of course, once it is in its final resting place, feel free to recycle the box and packaging.

A tip to get the case out of the box:

Open the top flaps of the box holding the case. Place one of the sides on the ground, making sure all the flaps are open.

Slowly turn the box upside down.

Lift the box to expose the case on the ground.

This saves you the hassle of trying to lift the case out of the box. It's much easier to lift a box, rather than the case!

With the case out, place it on the table or bench top that you are using for the build. Depending on the case that you use, there may be some extra steps you need to take to remove cross-bars and the like – consult your case manual for specifics ...

1. Remove case lid. There are usually one or two
   screws at the back of the lid.

2. Remove any loose cables, gel sacks, remotes, and
   bags of screws that are in the case. Note: they may
   be taped to a cross-member or side.

3. Position any attached cables to one side, out of
   the way (HDD light, power switch and reset switch
   cables).

4. From the motherboard box, take out the rear fascia and attach to the case.

   1.   Position the fascia inside the case facing to the rear.

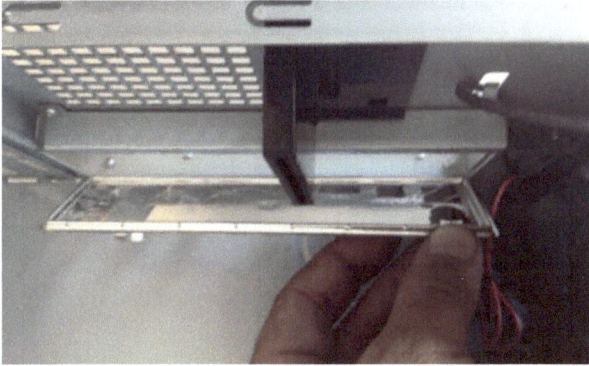

   2.   Make sure you have the fascia the right way around (and right way up)!

   3.   Once happy, push the four corners in until you hear them click into place.

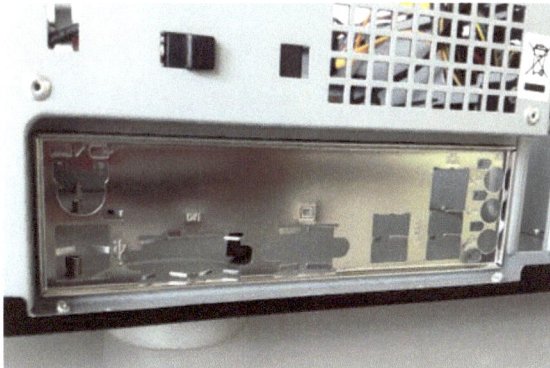

5. Take out your power supply and position it in the case. There are four bolt holes that will align with the back of the case.

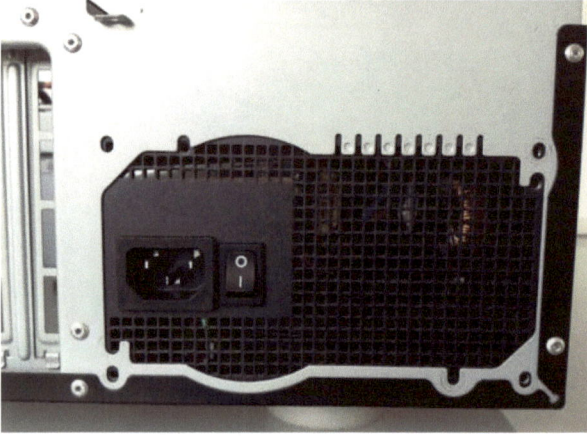

6. Screw the four screws that came with your power supply to lock it into place.

1. Depending on the power supply, you may need to plug in the cables that connect to the hard drives, optical drives, and GPU.

7. Unravel the power cables and position them so that they are out of the way.

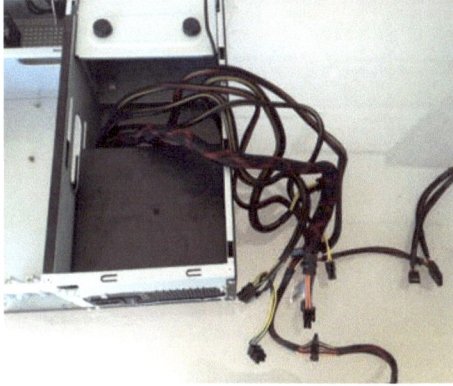

Now it is time to install the hard drives and optical drives into the case:

8. Take out the hard drive(s) and optical drive.

9. Position drives in the case drive bays, and fasten them with the supplied screws.

   1. Make sure the SATA ports are facing the back of the case.

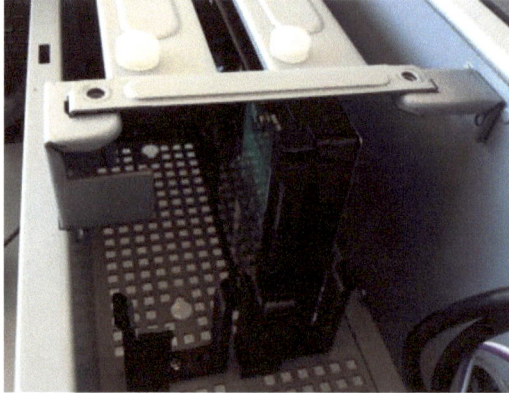

10. If required, make sure you add any motherboard mounting screws to the case.

   1. Get the pre-prepared motherboard from wherever you placed it earlier. Place it inside the case in the approximate position that it needs to be in.

2. Check to see if there are mounting screws in the location where the screws go through the motherboard – there are normally eight screws you need to worry about.

3. If you need to add a mounting screw, remove the motherboard and add the mounting screws as provided with the case.

11. Place the motherboard in the case.

1. Make sure the rear outputs line up with the fascia added in step 4.

2. Check that all of the earthing straps on the fascia are on top of the output terminals, NOT inside. This can be a particular problem for the ethernet / network terminal.

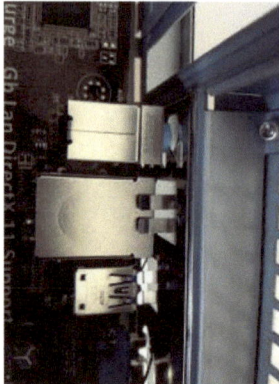

12. Align the screw holes on the motherboard with the mounting screws on the base of the case.

13. Fit the eight mounting screws to the motherboard.

　　1.　If you find it hard to locate the screws in the holes, trying using a pair of needle-nose pliers.Not essential, but definitely easier :)

　　2.　As an alternative, try using a magnetised screwdriver to hold the screw.

Cables

At this point, the main hardware is now installed inside the case, however none of it is connected, so now come the cables. Cables are generally designed to fit in only one way, so you don't have to worry about getting them aligned. Except for the first ones we'll discuss – let's start with the tricky ones first:

1. We need to attach the power button, power switch, HDD light, and reset switch. This is normally on the right hand side of the motherboard, viewing from back to front.

    1. Consult the motherboard manual to locate where, and what, orientation the cables need to be plugged into.

    2. The cables are two wires connected to a rectangular plug.

    3. Needle-nose pliers will make this job much easier.

    4. Not every case will have all four cables – just use the ones that you have got.

    5. Take your time – this is the most fiddly part of the build. Don't bend the pins.

2. Next is the main power cable. This is the big one (24 pins) coming from the power supply, and is made of many different colours of wire.

1. Feed the cable from the power supply to the motherboard.

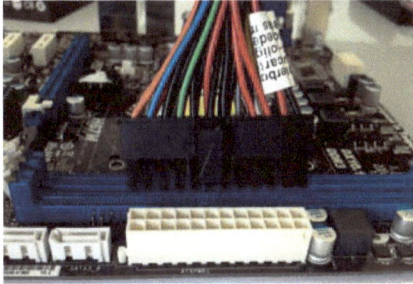

2. Align the cable with the power socket on the motherboard. There is a small clip that will hook into place on one side of the cable.

3. Press the cable down firmly until it clips into place.

3. The secondary power cable (known as the ATX power cable) is a similar process, except it is a smaller cable and is yellow and black:

1. The secondary power cable can either be 4, 6, or 8 pins. Check your motherboard manual to find out which applies to you.

2. Check the motherboard manual for the location of the secondary power socket on your motherboard.

4. Now, the on-board audio.

   1. Find the black plug from the case marked HD Audio.

   2. Use your motherboard manual to locate the HD Audio socket (also known as the Front Panel Audio socket) on the motherboard.

   3. The plug will only fit in one way – there is a blocked pin – you'll need to make sure it is properly aligned.

4. Press down to plug the cable into the socket.

5. Next is the USB and/or the IEEE (also known as 1394) cables.

   1. These are rectangular, and usually black.

2. Use the motherboard manual to locate the USB and/or IEEE sockets on the motherboard.

3.

Align the plug with the socket - it only fits one way due to a blocked pin – and press down to plug it in.

4. DO NOT MIX the USB and IEEE plugs. You can damage the motherboard.

6. Next, we connect the chassis fans to the pins on the motherboard.

1. Check the motherboard manual for plug locations.

2. Align the cable on the plug – they only fit one way.

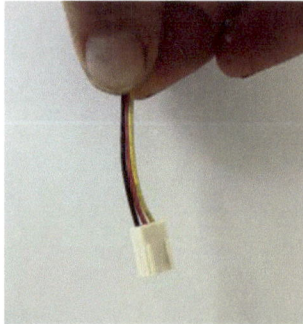

3. Press down to connect.

4. Depending on your case, you may have one, two, or three fans. Some cases have chassis fans that require connection to the main power supply. Check your case manual for further information.

7. Now, we connect the SATA data cables to the motherboard.

1. These only fit one way.

2. Make sure you connect the primary HDD (the one that will hold the operating system) to SATA port 1. This will prevent potential issues in future years when the motherboard battery runs out of power – the default boot port will revert back to SATA 1.

3. Connect the other end to each of your storage drives – both hard drives and optical drives.

4. If you have one end with a right angled connector, connect those to the drives. Use the flat connectors on the motherboard.

Finally, we connect the SATA power cables.

5. Connect the SATA power cable to the hard drives and optical drives.

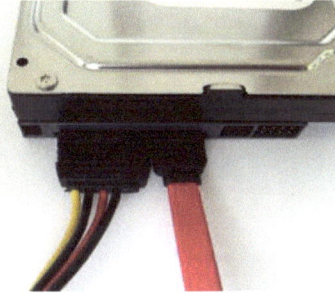

6. The other end will be connected to the power supply.

7. They only fit one way.

8. If you do not have enough SATA power cables, you can use an adaptor (see next section).

A quick word on adaptors. Sometimes, you will need to use a Molex to SATA power cable adaptor so that you can connect a SATA power cable to a spare Molex connector. When plugging in Molex connectors, you need to gently wiggle the two ends together to make sure the pins are aligned. It is easy to not have them aligned and then push, bending the pins. It's part of the reason we now use SATA.

Be careful and take your time. Remember: this is not a race.

PCI Cards

Now that the fiddly stuff is done, we have one last set of components to fit – the PCI cards. These will fit into the slots on the motherboard.

There are three basic types of PCI slots that you will find on your motherboard. These are:

1. PCI-Ex16 – graphic card slot. You may rarely come across AGP. Both these slots have a hook at the end to help hold the card in place and to prevent accidental removal.

2. PCI-E – standard card slot which most cards use.

3. PCI-Ex1 – the smaller card slot, becoming increasingly popular.

   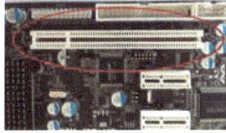   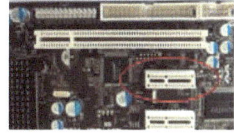

PCI-Ex16   *PCI-E*   *PCI-Ex1*

Depending on your system build, you may be installing anywhere from 1 to 6 PCI cards. Irrespective of which, or how many, cards the process is fundamentally the same:

1. Make sure there is no power connected to your media centre. Either unplug the power cable or ensure the power is switched off at the PSU.

2. Using your screwdriver, remove the PCI slot-guard screw at the back of the case.

3. Remove the PCI slot-guard.

4. Remove the PCI card from its protective bag.

5. Align the card with the correct slot.

6. Position the card in the slot. When happy with its position, press down firmly to push into place.

7.   Reattach the screw to lock the card into
        position.

Occasionally, case design and card design do not agree
– when you screw the card into place, it can move the
card in the slot. Generally this is not an issue, however
there are some precautions you can take to minimise any
issues:

1.   Always make sure there is no power
        connected to the motherboard when you
        install PCI cards. If the card moves when you
        screw it down, unwind the screw a little so
        that the card remains seated, yet still locked
        in by the screw.

2. In a worst case scenario, you can remove the screw, but be aware that the card may move when cables are being plugged into the back of it. As long as the media centre is powered off when you plug the cables in, it should not be a problem

3. In extremely rare cases, you might consider using a Dremil drill, or similar, to modify the card and /or case. I have only ever done this once, and I only recommend this for experienced builders if you have no other choice.

First Boot

Now it is time to plug it all in and fire up your new media centre! For the first boot, you only need the following items plugged in:

1.   The power cable, of course.

2.   A USB keyboard.

3.   A USB mouse.

4.   A monitor. You can use a standard, small computer monitor or your TV. Where possible use a HDMI connection, since that is what you will most likely use in your final configuration.

With everything plugged in, turn your monitor/TV on first. Then turn your media centre on. Depending on the brand of motherboard you use, and what BIOS it comes with, you will get a screen that looks a bit like this:

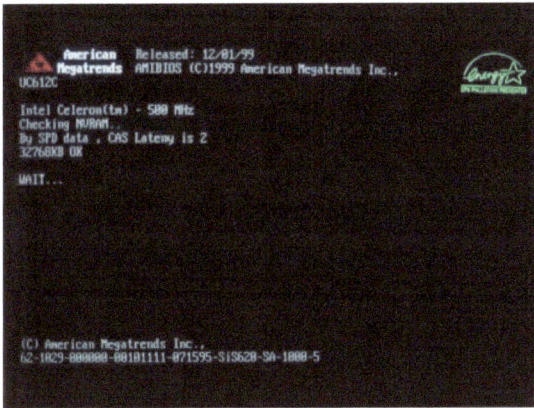

If you see this – congratulations! – everything is working. Now we need to set up the BIOS.

BIOS

Setting up the BIOS is something that must be done the first time that you boot up the media centre. BIOS (which stands for Basic Input Output Software) is the software that runs all the motherboard components before the operating system is loaded. Its primary function is to ensure that all the basic hardware is working OK and to get the computer ready to load the operating system.

To load the BIOS, you normally press <Del> key. Sometimes, it can be the <F2>. An instruction will always appear at the bottom of the boot screen the first time that you turn on your new media centre.

The BIOS screen will vary from computer to computer, based on the brand of BIOS and what features and components are built into the motherboard.

New Bios Screen   Older Bios Screen

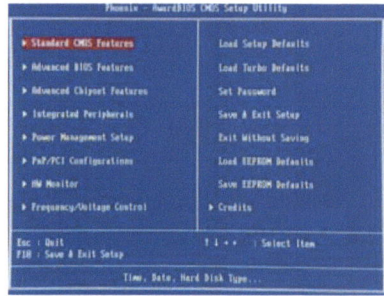

There are simply too many permutations to put into one book, let alone a chapter of a book, however there are some basics you need to look at:

1. Date and time.

2. Configuration of secondary graphics processors (ie: if you have an onboard GPU and a PCI GPU – you can choose which one is the default).

3. Fan speed settings. You normally have options to adjust the speed of the CPU and chassis fans – I recommend that you set them to silent for a media centre.

4. Check the boot priority. You can choose which drive boots first, ie: the CD/DVD ROM or the hard

drive. You can also determine which hard drive boots first if you have more than one.

NOTE: For the installation of the operating system, I recommend that you make the optical drive your first boot drive.

Navigating the BIOS is normally done with the keyboard arrow keys. Some of the newer BIOSs have mouse support enabled, but that's the exception rather than the rule.

Once you have made any changes that you want, you then save them and the system will reboot. Either navigate to the Exit or Save menu, or you can press <F10>.

If you aren't happy with the changes, you can always exit without saving.

The key messages here are:

1. Check your motherboard user guide (it's the book that comes with your motherboard) on exactly what setting details you have.

2. If you don't know what it does, don't change it.

Trouble Shooting

Sometimes things just don't go the way you planned. Although rare, there are times when your freshly built media centre won't fire up.

A) If you get no screen at all, check the following:

1. That the monitor or TV is plugged in. This is obvious, I know, but is worth checking.

2. That the media centre PSU is switched on. The switch is at the back of the power supply.

3. If you have more than one video source (ie: onboard and PCI graphics), try the other graphics ports.

B) If you get a screen, but the system keeps rebooting, check:

1. The RAM. Faulty RAM is a common cause of system reboots. Luckily, it is easy to fix – simply replace it.

C) If you get no screen and you can hear the fans starting up, then stopping, then starting up, then stopping, check:

1. The RAM. Faulty RAM is a common cause of system reboots. Luckily it is easy to fix – simply replace it.

D) Nothing happens at all:

1. Check the PSU, it may be faulty.

2. Try a larger specification PSU – there may not be enough power to start the system, especially if you are using a GPU that requires a PCI power connector, or if you are using multiple GPUs.

3. Try removing the GPU (if installed) and use the on-board GPU only.

4. Check the CPU compatibility with your motherboard. If it is not compatible, then the

motherboard will not start.

At this stage, these are the only problems you are likely to encounter.

Summary

We have now built our media centre! It's time to put on the lid and begin the software installation, but before we do, a couple of quick comments:

1. Take your time. Assembling your media centre is not a race – take your time and get it right.

2. Always refer to your motherboard manual. Every motherboard is different – and everything you need to know for the assembly phase is in the manual.

3. If you ever get stuck or are unsure:

    1. Go back and check this book for a bit of inspiration :)

    2. Do a Google search – you are not alone and someone, somewhere, will have come across the same problems you're facing.

Part 3

:: Software

What makes a media centre actually a media centre?

A media centre is something more than the sum of its parts. The hardware is essential, but by itself will not enable you to watch movies, listen to music, or record live TV.

The second phase of the build is the more complicated section – the software. There are two areas that will require your attention to detail to make sure you get the most out of your media centre:

The Operating System

The Media Centre Software

There is no right or wrong choice with either of these two elements, but you will need both, and deciding which choice to make can be very easy or very difficult. It all comes down to what you want and what you like to do.

In this section of the book, we will look at both of these elements – the operating system and the media centre software – in detail, and discover what the benefits of each are, as well as some of the pitfalls you can expect to encounter.

The right media centre software will make or break your media centre experience. This is because it is the software that you interface with. You don't communicate with the hardware – you use the software to do this for you. So, being comfortable with your media centre software is essential.

In all cases, the media centre software is designed to perform the basic functions of a media centre:

Watch and record live TV

Play movies

Play DVDs and/or Blu-ray discs

Listen to digital music

View and slideshow your picture collections

But there are other features that can add to your media centre experience:

Display current weather information

Show stock market information

Read and respond to emails

Social Media integration

Play internet radio

Customisation

Evolve with new technologies

Your choice of operating system and media centre software will govern how much flexibility you will have to modify and customise your media centre.

So, to answer the question "What makes a media centre?" - it is the software. That is what you interact with, and that is what makes your choices so important.

:: Operating Systems

Let's start with the operating system. There are three basic operating systems you can use:

Linux

Windows

Macintosh

We'll have a look at these individually and see what does, and does not, make each ideal for a media centre.

:: Macintosh

I am going to discount Macintosh right away. Mac users will flame me for this, but there are simple reasons why media centres are not made with Mac's. It is mostly to do with:

TV Tuners and live TV in general

The case

Macs, in particular Mac Minis - do not give you the ability to install third party hardware. This limits your TV tuner type to USB only. Although it will work, USBs are not the preferred tuner for a permanent media centre. They are great for a mobile solution, or when you will be using the computer for other purposes, ie, a laptop.

Secondly, a Mac does not come in any other case other than the one from the factory. Again this limits how your media centre will look. Personally, I think that a media centre should be a dedicated machine that looks like a piece of home theatre equipment. A Mac, as lovely as they are, does not fit in visually with the rest of your home theatre equipment.

Thirdly, there are no real options for dedicated media centre software. Plex is the only real option, and I will discuss why this is not ideal later in this section.

:: Windows

Windows is the world's most popular operating system. According to W3School, around 83-85% of all computers run a Windows operating system. Over 50% are Windows 7. Why is this important for a media centre?

Firstly, is driver development. With the bulk of the world's computers running a Windows operating system, you can bet that the first driver that is released is a Windows one. Why would a manufacturer turn away 80% of their potential market? They don't. Windows drivers are always the first developed and always in the first release.

Secondly, there is an enormous user base, which means that are lots of people who use the operating system and a number of those will gladly share their knowledge with you. The upshot of this is that there is a LOT of information available on the web about Windows operating systems.

If you have a problem with your Windows machine, you can bet that someone else has also experienced it and probably solved it. And it is also likely that they have shared their solution via the web. This makes trouble shooting far easier.

Windows is a very easy to use operating system. You

insert the installation CD, answer a few questions and 15-20 minutes later, you have a fully installed operating system. It means that you don't need a lot of computer knowledge to get started. In fact, you don't really need any computer knowledge at all.

Add to this that most people use a Windows operating system at work, or have family members that do – it makes Windows an intuitive operating system. You just know how to use it, as virtually everyone does.

It's Not All Good

Those are some major positives, but it is not all peaches and cream. Windows is expensive and is another cost to your media centre. If you are on a budget, this can be a problem.

It is a 'closed' operating system, meaning that only Microsoft developers are able to access and modify the operating system code. This locks you into having the resources and functionality that they give you.

Being the most popular operating system also makes it the target for hackers, viruses, and other nasty things, that can potentially destroy your system. You need protection which can affect your media centre's performance.

Windows does not come with many codecs. Codecs are the files that you need to playback various media files. To play an MP3 song, you need a MP3 codec. To play a DivX movie, you need a DivX codec. Windows does not come with a DivX codec, so you need to find a third party codec to be able to play it. We will discuss codecs in more detail later in the book.

Finally, Windows will not play Blu-ray movies. There are commercial reasons for this, but as a media centre owner, you don't care. In fact, it took a long time for Windows to play DVDs natively. You can't do it in Windows XP and only the higher-end version of Vista. In fact, Windows 8 lost native DVD playback, something that Windows 7 was able to do.

:: Linux

Linux makes up only 5% of the world's operating systems, however it is used extensively in the education, engineering, and computer science areas. This gives it a very dynamic user base of dedicated and knowledgeable people who are usually very willing to help people to 'come over from the dark side'.

Linux is a 'free' operating system that is issued under the GNU licence agreement. This means you can download it free from a variety of sources, and install it on as many systems as you like. The reason it is free is because it is developed and maintained by a group of people who volunteer their time and resources into improving and developing the operating system.

This is one of Linux's core strengths – its flexibility and freedom. If you wanted, you could re-write the code and issue your own version! This is the principle behind the GNU project – free software for all, as long as the source code is shared and credited accordingly.

Because Linux comes in many 'flavours', I am not going to list them all. I will mention that Ubuntu is the version best suited for a media centre. It is popular, well-developed, and is the operating system of choice for one of the two preferred media centre software packages discussed in the next chapter.

The other core strength of Linux is its customisability. If you have the knowledge and/or desire, you can change everything about Linux. You can even rewrite the kernel source code if you want to. This flexibility means you can fine tune every aspect of your media centre experience, as you want to. The reality is that you don't need to – because Linux is a highly developed, intuitive operating system.

Pretty much anything you can do on a Windows or Macintosh machine, you can do in Linux for free.

The Drawbacks

The reality is though, that only 5% of the computing world uses Linux. This means two things:

1. Driver development is slower than that for Windows

2. There is no official support for Linux

The lack of general acceptance of Linux has slowed the driver development rate. Most companies will focus on producing drivers for the bulk of their market first – and this means Windows. Linux drivers usually come later, especially if it is a smaller company.

This is not a real problem if you aren't going to be using the newest hardware, but if you are, you need to check for driver availability before you shell out your cold hard cash for new components.

By official support, I mean being able to ring up a call centre and get help. Given that the development is carried out largely by volunteers, there is ro direct support. Having said that, the online support is fantastic. Chances are that if you are having a problem, someone else will have already encountered it, fixed it, improved the code, and blogged or commented all about it in a forum.

Linux is very much an operating system that you learn about, and teach yourself.

:: So Which Should You Choose?

There is no right or wrong answer to this question. The real question is:

What are you used to?

My recommendation is that you stick with what you know. It will help with trouble shooting any issues you might encounter along the way. It will also put you in your comfort zone, which is a great place to be when you're learning something new.

But if you like a challenge and enjoy learning new things, try the operating system that you don't know. For most of you, that will mean Linux. It is a great operating system and is fun to learn!

If you are still unsure on which to choose, here is a list of the pros and cons of each:

	Windows	Linux	Mac Os
Cost	$$$	Free	$$$
Driver Support	Best	Good	OK
Online Support	Great	Great	Good
Phone Support	Great	N/a	Great
Flexibility	Limited	High	Minimal
Software Availability	High	High	Medium
Ease of Use	High	Medium	High

If you still can't decide, I recommend that you use Windows. It does cost more to install, but you will never miss out on driver development and there will always be support and help available should you need it.

:: Media Centre Software

There are quite a few media centre software packages available. Most of them are free (or close too it), so which one should you use?

The answer to that question partially depends on which operating system you choose. Let's look at some of the media centre software options available, discuss the pros and cons of each, and which operating systems they work with.

Windows Media Centre

The first one we'll look at is the inbuilt media centre that comes bundled with Microsoft Windows, at least it was with Windows Vista and Windows 7. In Windows 8, you need to purchase the Media Centre upgrade to enable its functionality.

The Windows Media Centre is a highly polished media centre that has been in development for some time. The first version became available in Windows XP as a special edition called – wait for it – Windows XP Media Centre Edition. Since then, it has been developed by the considerable resources available to Microsoft to become the easiest media centre to use on the market.

It also comes with a built-in ability to use your TV tuner, provided one is installed, which is something that cannot be said for all the others. To me, the TV tuner is a core part of any media centre, even if you don't watch much TV at all. As of Windows 7, Electronic Program data (EPG) is downloaded from the TV signal and displayed in the media centre natively. This enables you to set up scheduled recordings and season pass recordings with ease.

The user interface is extremely smooth and intuitive to use. Even my three year old can pick up the remote and start navigating the cross-hair navigation system to find what she wants. The scrolling is very smooth and everything can be done with the remote.

The biggest single advantage that Windows Media Centre has over all the others is the ability to add extenders. Extenders are slave devices that stream media from the main media centre so that it can be displayed on another screen in a totally separate location. This 'extends' the functionality of the media centre into other rooms in your house. Microsoft has this functionality firmly cornered – the best extender on the market is the Xbox 360, and it comes with the extender software built-in. Extenders can also be set up in XBMC, but it is a much more complicated process.

Nevertheless, Windows Media Centre (WMC) does have some drawbacks. Most notably is the inability to play most codecs natively. Windows Vista and Windows 7 will play DVDs natively, however the latest version shipped with Windows 8 does not. WMC will not play many DivX files natively, nor is it capable of playing MKV or flac files.

The WMC user interface is not customisable. You can't change the default colour from blue, and you can't move menu items around and group programs together. You can't change the order of the menu items either. In short, you can't really do anything to the interface – one of the drawbacks of using a closed or locked piece of software.

Another problem people find with WMC is the inability to sort music by folder. Like iTunes, the music can only be sorted using meta tags. This is fine for songs downloaded from iTunes, but ripped CDs and hard-to-get albums, not to mention DJ mixes often haveno meta tags. This makes it difficult to navigate using the built-in music section. This can become a real pain in the backside if you have a large music collection (like mine which currently stands at 100+ GB). In fact, some music will not show up at all because there are no meta tags – lossless flac files, for example.

A fundamental drawback with WMC is that, although WMC will find and download album cover art, it won't do it for movies or ripped DVDs. A ripped DVD (or CD for that matter) is a DVD that you have copied the entire contents of onto your media centre to allow you to play it back without using the optical disc.

Given the closed nature of the source code for Windows Media Centre, the development of plug-ins is quite slow. There are some great plug-ins out there, but there are not many plug-ins in general, and many of the ones that are available are not updated frequently.

Finally, Windows Media Centre is only available on the Windows operating system. If you plan to use, or are using Macintosh or Linux, then you will not be able to use Windows Media Centre.

There are ways around all of these issues (except the last one), and there are plug-ins that will do most of the work for you, as long as you know which ones to use – something we will look at in Part 4.

XBMC

XBMC is the main alternative to Windows Media Centre. It was originally developed as an alternative media centre for the original Xbox. Several media centre projects were merged together and released to the public in 2002 – the start of XBMC development. Eventually, the project grew to point that it was ported to the Linux operating system and this is where it has been based ever since.

The user interface in XBMC is very good. Like Windows Media Centre, the user interface is very slick and well developed. The navigation system is more linear, more like a web page where you have a high level navigation that is left-to-right with a second level menu underneath it.

XBMC is highly customisable. You can basically change anything if you have the skill to do so. But even if you don't, you can change the 'skin' – the look and feel of the media centre very easily. You can even download pre-made skins that other professional designers have made that look super cool. Many of these are themed, so if you like princesses and pink castles you can get that as your media centre theme. If you are a Transformers fan, then you can have a Transformers theme, etc...

This customisability is extended to plug-ins and apps. There are many plugins available for the XBMC media centre. For example, one of my favourites is the DI.FM plugin. This plugin gives me access to all the Digitally Imported web radio channels within XBMC, meaning that I can use the remote to quickly and easily select and play my favourite DI.FM radio channel. There are many more plugins you can explore.

XBMC is released under the GNU licence agreement, therefore the source code is readily available. This means that there is continuous development of not only the core, but the plugins too. The upshot of this, is that XBMC is constantly updated and improved. As technology develops, XBMC develops with it.

Codec support is another great strength of XBMC. XBMC will play just about anything you throw at it, natively. DVDs, MKVs, flac, WMV – XBMC can handle them all. XBMC uses the FFDshow codec package to provide this play back functionality – and FFDshow is also continuously developed. Blu-ray is the only thing that XBMC will not handle natively, but I will show you how to enable this functionality later in the book.

It is also noteworthy that XBMC is available across all major platforms including Linux, Windows, Macintosh (OSX), and even as a bootable version on a USB stick. This means that you can use XBMC on just about ANY computer, given that the minimal specs are met.

However, there are drawbacks. Most notably is the lack of TV tuner support by default. XBMC will not natively access TV tuners installed in your media centre, nor will it be able to download the EPG data for season pass recordings.

XBMC does not come with RC6 remote support out of the box. RC6 remotes are the standard IR remotes that are used in media centres. Almost every remote on the market uses the RC6 codes.

Then there is the setup process. This is not as smooth or intuitive as Windows Media Centre. The actual install itself is reasonably straightforward, but then you need to install several small programs on top of the media centre to enable the remote and the TV tuners – the most basic of functions required for any media centre.

If you use the Linux operating system, or like to customise and play around with your media centre software, then XBMC is the media centre software for you.

Plex

Plex is an alternative to XBMC. In fact, it is a development of XBMC, and as such, many of the features, functionality, and add-ons from XBMC have carried over to Plex. So, what are the differences between Plex and XBMC?

There are some significant differences and some less noticeable ones. Firstly is the licencing. Plex is a mostly closed source program. This means that the core of the media centre is not available for the public to edit and tinker/improve. XBMC is totally open source and anyone can modify and play with the source code as they see fit. From a user perspective, this is irrelevant – as long as it works.

The second difference is that because Plex is effectively 'closed source', there is less development of Plex than there is of XBMC. Again, this is not a major issue for users, but is worth noting.

Of more significance is the fact that Plex was developed almost specifically for Macintosh (OSX). This makes it the primary choice for Mac users, although XBMC is now available for Macs too.

Plex is essentially a media server with clients that run on secondary machines (or on the server machine if you wish). This is a significant difference in the way Plex operates in comparison to XBMC.

It basically means that Plex clients can be installed on far less powerful machines (say an Apple TV) because the client doesn't need to do any decoding. All this is done on the Plex Media Server – a single 'master' machine that is built for this specific purpose.

XBMC is installed as a standalone piece of software which means lower-powered machines are not able to cope.

In essence, there is little visual difference between Plex and XBMC. However, if you are using a Mac for your media centre, then Plex is the preferred media centre software because it was originally developed for Macs.

The Others

You will come across a number of other media centre software packages, like MythTV, Media Portal, and Media Browser, to name a few. All of these media centre programs have something to offer, however as overall packages, they are not suited to the general media centre user.

The reasons I do not discuss them in detail are two-fold. All the other media centre software packages fail on one of two accounts:

1. They are too complicated to install, and generally require the use of a mouse early on

2. They lack key functionality (either no TV support, or clunky user interface, etc...)

Therefore, I will not say any more on these, other than to say that there are other options out there if you want to explore them. A simple Google search will reveal where you can download them from and some instructions on installation.

	Windows	Linux	Macintosh (OSX)
Windows Media Centre	✓		
XBMC	✓	✓	✓
Plex	✓	✓	✓
Media Portal	✓	✓	
MediaBrowser	✓	✓	
MythTV		✓	

Summary

So, which media centre software package should you use? Again, stick with what you know. If you are a Windows user, I recommend that you use Windows Media Centre. If you are a Linux user, I recommend that you start with XBMC. If you insist on using a Mac, then Plex is your only real option.

However, if you are a bit more experienced, or like to explore, I do encourage you to try other media centre software packages. You will discover things that you like and things you dislike about all the packages – and that is half the fun of building your own media centre!

Given that the best options are WMC and XBMC, I will cover the installation of these two. Aside from these two media centre packages being the best at what they do, you will also spend far less time fixing problems. They both work, and work well. The other options available are either too complex to set up or don't do everything in one package.

:: Setting Up Your Media Centre

Now that you have built the hardware of your media centre, and installed the components and the basic operating system, it is time to 'build' and set up the software part of your media centre. This can take some time, depending on how far you want to go.

In this section, we will cover the initial software setup required to get you up and running. At the end of this build process, you will be able to:

- Watch and record live TV
- Watch an optical disc (DVD)
- Watch an avi or mkv video
- Play music from your CD collection
- Play downloaded music, including MP3s, flac, and aac files
- Create slideshows of your favourite pictures

In Part 4, we will look at additional plugins that will make your media centre experience even better – including how to set up your media centre to watch Blu-ray movies.

:: Windows Media Centre

Given that most machines have Windows installed, I will start with the Windows Media Centre. I highly recommend Windows 7 Home Premium as your operating system for this. Most of what will be discussed will also apply to Windows Vista, and to a slightly lesser degree, Windows XP Media Centre edition. If you have Windows XP Media Centre edition, I strongly encourage you to upgrade to Windows 7. There are some fundamental features that are worth the extra money:

- Over the air EPG data is downloaded in Windows 7 & 8

- Native DVD playback (not available by default in Windows 8)

At this point, the assumptions are that you have:

- All your hardware installed on the media centre (TV tuners, GPU, etc...)

- You have installed the operating system (Windows 7)

This is what is called a 'vanilla' installation. It's plain and needs to be 'flavoured' to your liking.

Drivers

Drivers are the bits of software that allow the operating system to talk to the various bits of hardware. This includes the TV tuner, the processor, and even your USB ports. If you do not have a driver installed for a particular component, then you will not be able to use it. This makes drivers very important!

So, the first thing you need to do is install the drivers for your hardware. Windows will have installed some basic drivers, but it is best to use the drivers from the manufacturer where possible. They will be more up-to-date, product specific, and in some cases, will have more features available.

There are two sources for drivers:

> The installation CD
> The manufacturer's website

Where possible, it is best to get the drivers from the manufacturer's website as they will be the latest, most stable (usually), and most feature-rich. The ones on the CD are older and don't always deal with some of the problems that early users have faced.

The process for installation is quite straightforward. Let's follow the process using the CD you received with your hardware:

1. Insert CD into drive.

2. Allow the autostart function to pop up. This will ask you if you want to run the setup file. Click the setup file to run it (if you do not have the autostart function on then open Computer from the Start menu and navigate

to the CD drive – usually D – and run the main program there).

3.   Follow the prompts from the installation program. Unless you have a specific reason to do otherwise, use the default settings.

4.   At the end of a driver installation (which can take several minutes), you may be asked to restart your computer. I usually wait until I have installed all of my drivers before I do the restart.

The order that you do the driver install is not very important, however there are some things you will need drivers for before you can do much else. The obvious example is the Network Interface Card (NIC for short). This is the bit that connects you to a network, and therefore the internet. Here is the order of driver installation that I recommend:

1.   Motherboard drivers (also known as chipset drivers). You don't have to install the other additional software from their installation CD, in fact I would recommend that you don't unless you know what you are doing.

Generally, they are designed for people who over-clock their machines – something we will not be doing. The motherboard driver will cover RAM, CPU, USB, the on-board network card, and anything else that is part of the motherboard. This can include the embedded graphics, if present.

2.   Graphics driver. If you are using an Nvidia or ATI-Radeon graphics card, then download the latest drivers from their websites. They both have a 'detect and install' plugin that will automatically determine what hardware you have and which is the best driver for it. If you have an embedded graphics chip, then you have already installed a driver in Step 1. It is still worth checking the embedded graphics manufacturer's website for the latest driver.

3.   Any other cards you might be using. This can include audio cards, USB hubs, etc...

4.   The IR receiver. Whatever IR or RF receiver you are going to use, you will need to install it so the media centre can be controlled by your remote. iMon is a popular choice. Download the latest stable driver from the IR/RF receiver manufacturer's website and install.

5.   The TV tuners. If you have not yet done so, install the TV tuner drivers. Usually the ones on the CD are adequate – TV tuner drivers are not often updated. Be wary of their third party TV recorders. You don't want to install these as you won't be using them, and they will slow your system down unnecessarily.

Then, restart your media centre to make sure it all works.

Windows Update

Now that we have all the drivers installed – including the NIC (Network Interface Card) – we can now make sure Windows is up-to-date.

To do this, we need to open Windows Update and get it to check our system, and then download any updates that are required.

1. Click on the Start button at the bottom left of your screen.

2. Type in "Windows Update" and press enter. A list of programs will come up and Windows Update will be highlighted. Pressing Enter simply opens it.

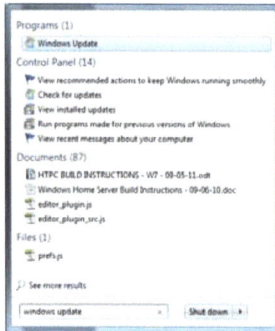

3. Click on Install Updates to start the process.

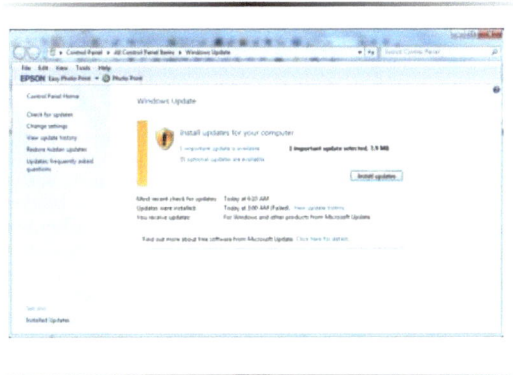

From here on, it is mostly an automated process. You may be asked to allow an install to occur. Obviously, say yes – they are all Microsoft products here, so there is no risk to your media centre.

Once the updates are completed, you will most likely have to reboot your system. When the media centre restarts, run Windows Update again and repeat the above process.

You may need to do this 3 or 4 times, depending on your system and what operating system you are installing. Keep repeating this process until there are no more important updates to install.

The updates can take some time. Be prepared with a cup of tea, coffee, or whatever floats your boat.

Also, be aware that these updates can be quite large. For example, a Service Pack (which is a bunch of updates all rolled into one package) can be over 500MB. Make sure you have sufficient download capacity before you start. You will only need to do this process during the installation. Once your media centre is running nicely, there is little need to run updates. UNLESS:

1. You use your media centre to surf the internet

2. You perform any tasks other than watching/ listening to media (ie, emails, using Word, Excel, etc...)

In such cases, you should run updates regularly (monthly) to make sure your system is protected and up-to-date.

Codecs

The next step is brought about by the biggest issue with Windows Media Centre: codecs. Codec is short for Coder-Decoder. A codec is the bit of software that enables the media centre to decode the digital video and audio media, and turn it into something you can see and hear.

By default, Windows Media Centre has limited codec support. It will play DVDs natively, along with MP3s, CDs, avi's and wmv files. However, its won't play Blu-ray, MKV, flac and ogg files, and DivX or Xvid files. So, we need to install a codec package to supplement Windows 7s shortcomings.

There are two main codec packs:

1. Shark Codecs
2. K-Lite

There are many other packs on the internet, however, I am only going to recommend one – The Shark Codec package. I use this one personally because:

1. There is no 'player' bundled with it – making it a smaller install.

2. It is continuously developed.

3. There is a good forum for troubleshooting, should you need it.

4. It is normally the first to bring new technologies to your media centre (like DTS Master Audio).

5. There is a 'Sharks Recommended Settings' button that automates the codec configuration.

6. It has a dedicated 64-bit codec package.

Download the Windows 7 or Windows 8 codec package from http://www.shark007.net as required. If you are using a 64-bit operating system (and you should be), then make sure you download both the 32-bit <u>and</u> 64-bit versions. Install the 32-bit codec package. Make sure you do so with Administrator privileges. Do this by right-clicking on the installation file and selecting "Run as administrator".

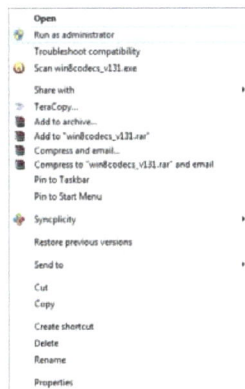

If you are logged in as the administrator (ie, you only have one user account on your media centre), then the User Account Control dialogue box will come up asking if you are sure that you want to install it. Click 'Yes' and it will install.

If you are not logged in as an Administrator, then you will be asked for the Admin account name and password. Fill these out and then follow the prompts to install.

If you are using a 64-bit operating system, then repeat the above process with the 64-bit codec package as well.

Once the codec packages have been installed, you will need to do some minor configuration, which will consist of a few button clicks. You can do this by following the steps as below:

1. Click on Start and type in 'settings'. The list of programs that comes up in the start menu will include 'Settings Application x64'. RIGHT CLICK on this and choose 'Run as administrator'.

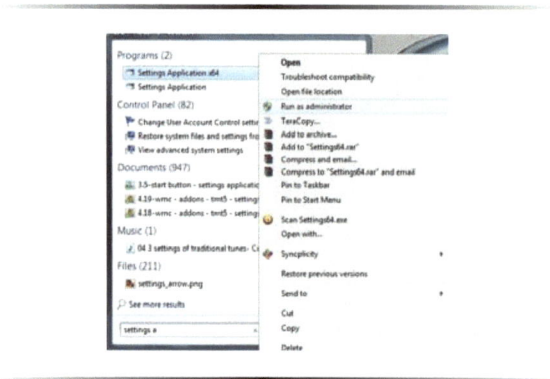

2. After the usual UAC dialogue box, you will be presented with the configuration dialogue box.

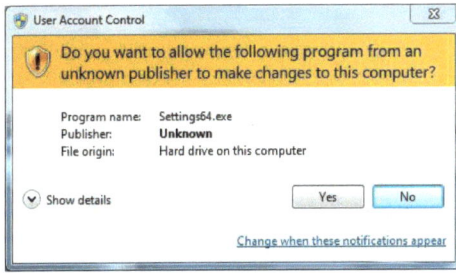

3.   Click on the 'Config' tab.

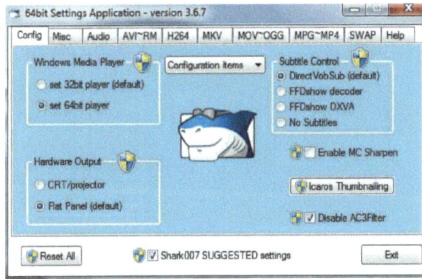

4.   In the 'Windows Media Player', click the 'set 64-bit player'.

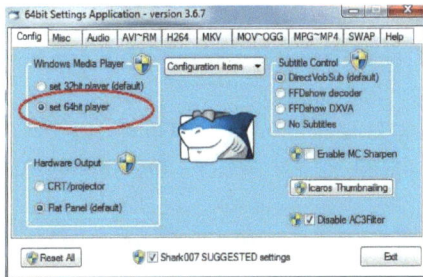

5.   At the bottom of the window, select the 'Shark007 SUGGESTED settings'.

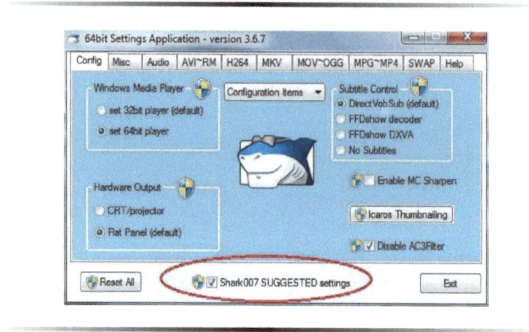

6.   Click the 'Audio' tab.

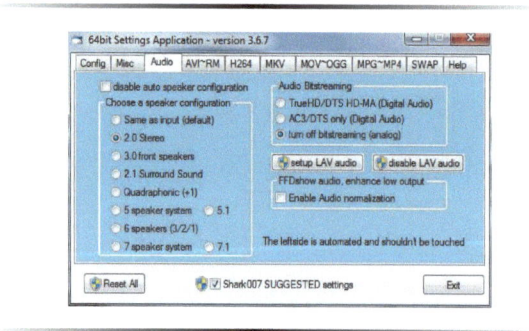

7.   Under the 'Audio Bitstreaming' section, choose which of the three settings is appropriate for you:

1. 'turn off bitstreaming' is for analogue audio – we won't be using this.

2. 'AC3/DTS only' is for Audio Visual Receivers (AVR) that do not support high-definition lossless audio. These are generally older AVRs with HDMI. This is also the setting if you are using an

152

optical connection for your audio.

3. 'TrueHD/DTS HD-MA' is the preferred setting if your AVR will decode lossless audio, like Dolby True HD and DTS High Definition-Master Audio.

8.   Click the Exit button to save your settings.

These settings will enable playback of virtually any media file you are likely to come across.

Restart your media centre before we begin the next section.

Once your media centre has rebooted, it is time to plug in your TV antenna (if you haven't already done so), so we can start putting the finishing touches on your Windows Media Centre.

Windows Media Centre Configuration

After rebooting your media centre, start the Windows Media Centre. In Windows 7:

1. Click on the Start button in the bottom left corner of your screen.

2. Click on "Windows Media Centre". If you can't see Windows Media Centre, click on "All Programs' and scroll down until you find it. Look for this logo:

In Windows 8, slide across the mosaic until you find the Windows Media Centre icon. Remember that you will need to purchase the Media Centre Pack (or have the Windows Ultimate edition) to get this icon. It looks like this:

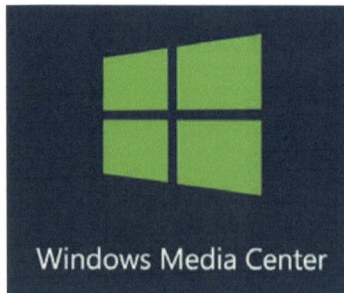

Now that Windows Media Centre has started, we need to configure the media centre to receive the correct TV signal types and to allocate the tuners to do the TV playback and recording. Once this step is done, you will have a fully functional Windows Media Centre.

When Windows Media centre starts, you will be greeted with the 'Welcome to Windows Media Centre' screen. Click 'Continue' to, well, continue.

You will then be asked if you want to use the Express setup (recommended) or the Custom setup. The Express setup will try and set the media centre up using your current locale. This may involve a small download to see if it can setup TV guides and so on. Click Express to continue.

The next stage is to set up the TV signal for your media centre. This is a 'follow-your-nose' process. Simply follow the on-screen instructions. Select 'Live TV Setup'.

Using your current Windows 7 settings, you will be shown your current region. If this is correct then select 'Next'. If not, select 'I want to use another region' and you will be shown a list of countries you can choose.

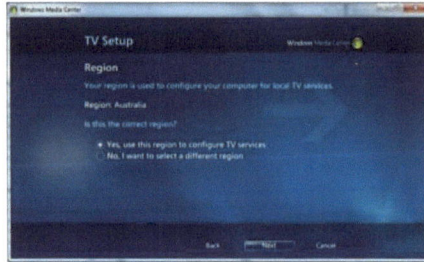

You then need to enter a postcode or zipcode. If you live in the US, it will attempt to download a TV guide package for you. If you live outside the US, it will tell you that there is no data available. That's fine, click 'Next'.

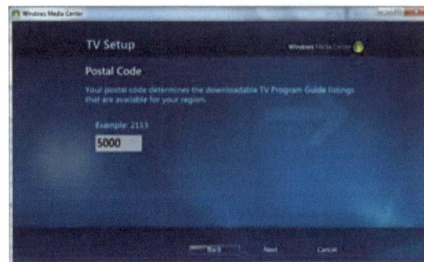

Agree to the terms of service. If you choose 'I do not agree', the TV setup process will stop.

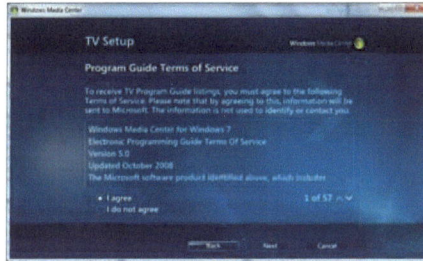

Then agree to install PlayReady. PlayReady is a form of DRM (Digital Rights Management) and a collection of Microsoft supported codecs. Basically, it will allow you to watch WMV, AAC, and H.264 encoded content. Since we already have codecs covered with the Shark007 Codec pack, we don't need it, but in order to continue, we have to agree so that we can move on.

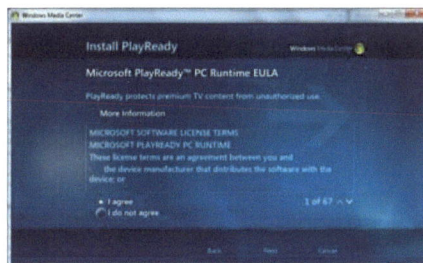

It will then either download the data (if in the US), or try to download the data (outside of the US). Either way, click 'Next' to start setting up the tuners:

157

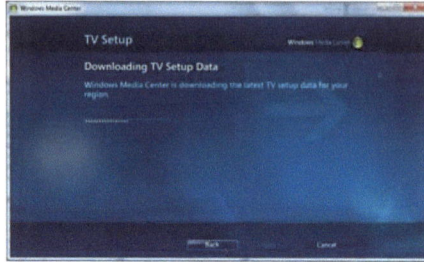

Now we have to choose which method we are receiving our TV signal with. For most people, it will be via antenna. If you have cable TV and a card using a QAM TV tuner, use the cable option. Similarly, if you are using a satellite TV tuner card, then select satellite.

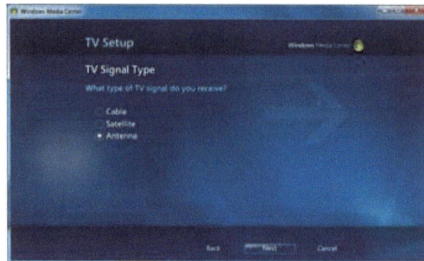

Then we need to identify if we are using a set-top box. Usually, the answer is No, unless you are using Foxtel (or similar), in which case you would choose Yes.

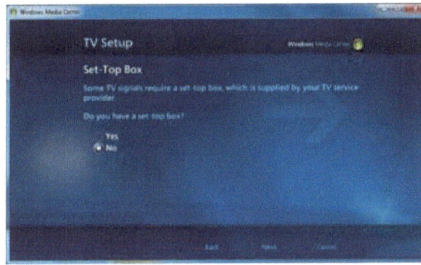

Then choose Analogue or Digital TV signal. You will almost exclusively need to select Digital Antenna (DVB-T).

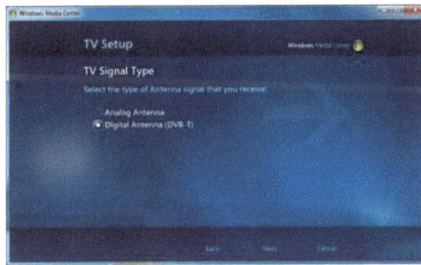

Now, we confirm which tuners we will be using:

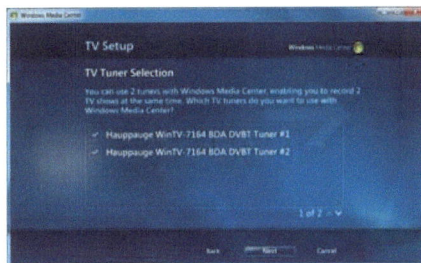

At this point, the TV tuners are set up. If you have a hybrid tuner, and you want to set up the analogue (FM) tuner, you can select Yes, otherwise choose No, so that we can start the scanning process.

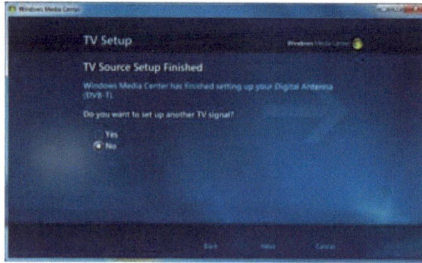

You will get a confirmation screen to that effect.

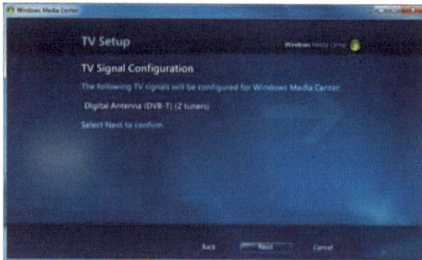

The system will now start scanning for guide data (which will fail outside the US).

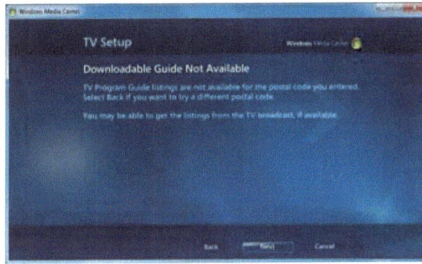

Finally, we start the scan for TV channels:

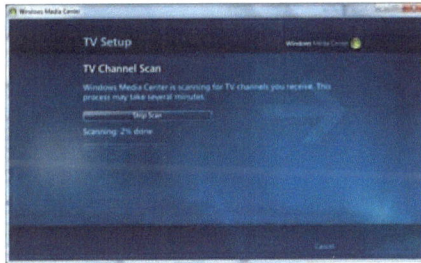

When the scan is complete, you will see a list of TV stations that have been picked up:

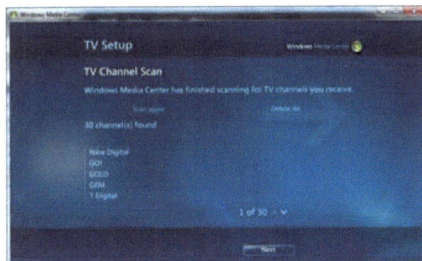

And now you are done!

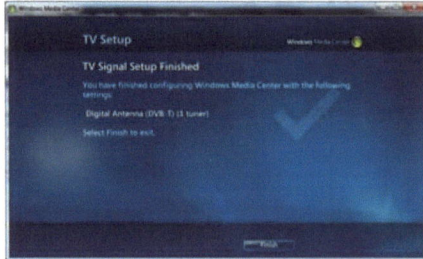

Congratulations!

You have now successfully set up your very own media centre! But wait ... there's a little more to do.

Set Up Windows Media Centre Libraries

In order to be able to play your music collection, movie files, and ripped DVDs, we need to tell the Media Centre where to look for the files. There are two ways to do this – one is by using the remote control inside the media centre; the other is to use your keyboard and mouse in the Windows 7 desktop.

:: Using the Mouse and Keyboard

This is the easiest and fastest way to set up the media

libraries. To do this, we need to close the Windows Media Centre and return to the desktop. Do this with your mouse by clicking the red cross at the top right.

1.	Click Start and then open Computer (right handside of Start menu).

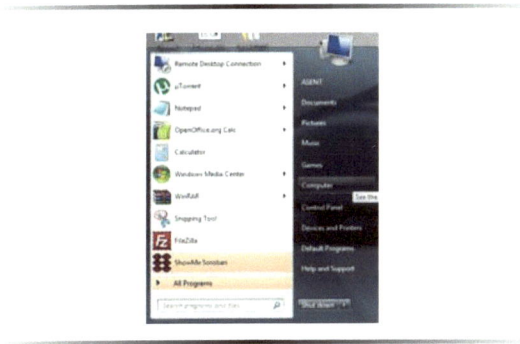

2.	In the left hand pane of Computer, you will see the Libraries. This will include Videos, Music, and Pictures.

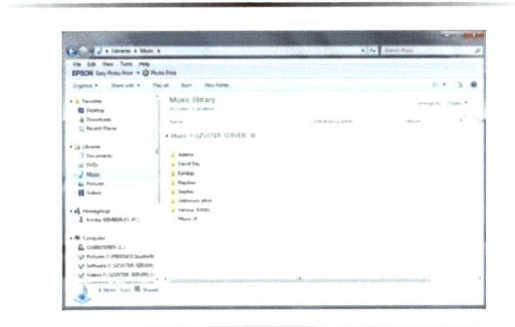

3.   Click on Videos. The right-hand pane will now show the music library with some standard content that comes with your Windows 7 installation.

4.   At the top of the Video library is a link which says 'Includes: 2 locations' (the actual number may vary – it's the link that is important). The word locations will be blue – like an internet hyperlink. Click on the word 'locations'.

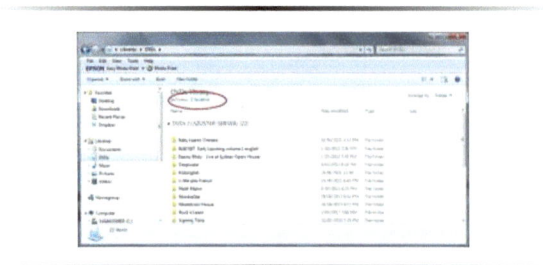

5.   A dialogue box will come up showing you the locations that are currently set as the Video library. You will notice that you can Add or Remove locations by using the buttons on the right-hand side.

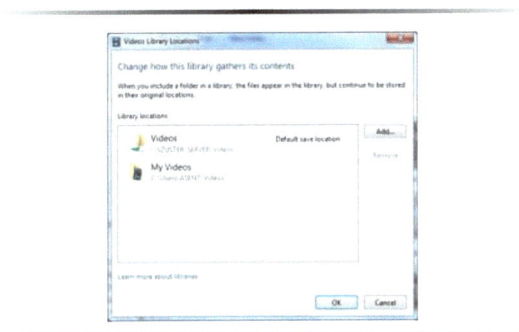

6.   Click the 'Add' button and select the folder you would like to add to the Video library.

A word on media folders. I strongly recommend that you install two hard drives – one for the media centre, the other for your media. The media drive should be as large as possible – at least 1Tb. On the media drive, I recommend that you create at least five folders:

1.   Videos
2.   Music
3.   Pictures
4.   DVDs
5.   Recorded TV

You can then put your various media files into the appropriate folder. This will make it easy to manage your collection of media as it grows. And it will grow!

7.   Click 'include folder' to – you guessed it –
            include the folder.

8.   Once you have added all the folders that
            you want to your Video library, be sure
            to delete the original ones. If you don't,
            the media centre may start filling those
            folders with your media, which will make it
            hard to find later on.

            1. Select the location to delete.

            2. Click the Remove button.

You then repeat this process for the Music and Picture libraries.

If you look at the Computer folder again, you will see on the left-hand pane, a grouping at the top called 'Favourites'. In this grouping, you will find a location called 'Recorded TV'. You need to carry out the steps above for this Recorded TV library as well.

Finally, we need to create a library for our ripped DVDs.

1.   In 'Computer', click on the Libraries grouping in the left-hand pane.

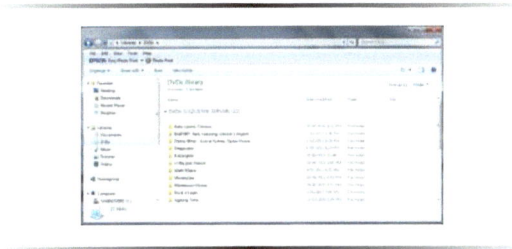

2.   On the menu above the Libraries listing, on the right-hand pane, click on 'New Library'.

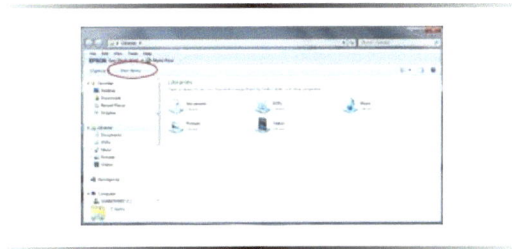

3.   Give the new library a name. I recommend 'DVDs'.

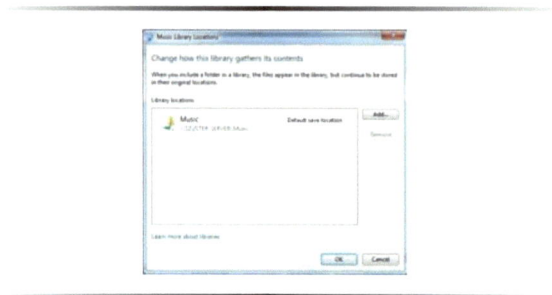

4.   Repeat the process above for adding any other folders for the library.

Once we have done this, Windows Media Centre will automatically look at these media libraries and show you what is there. All you have to do is add your new media to the media libraries and you'll see it in your Media Centre right away.

:: Using the Remote

If using the keyboard and mouse is not your cup of tea, then you can do a very similar process using the remote.

The first thing to note is that it is still important to set up the file structure of your media hard drive in an easy to follow, logical manner. Rehashing what we covered before:

"A word on media folders. I strongly recommend that you install two hard drives – one for the media centre, the other for your media. The media drive should be as large as possible – at least 1Tb. On the media drive I recommend you create at least five folders:

1. Videos
2. Music
3. Pictures
4. DVDs
5. Recorded TV

You can then put your various media files in the appropriate folder. This will make it easy to manage your collection of media as it grows. And it will grow!"

So, assuming that you have already done this – and you should have – we'll now use the remote to tell the media centre where to look for video files.

Like a lot of functions in the Windows Media Centre, there are two ways to get to the 'Add a folder' process.

1.   Use the remote to navigate to the Tasks menu and select 'Settings'.

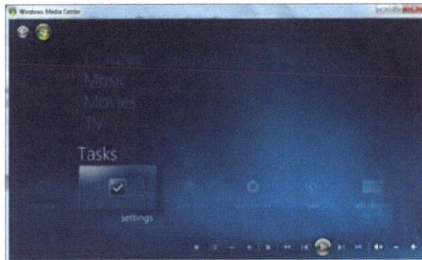

2.   Choose Media Libraries from the menu.

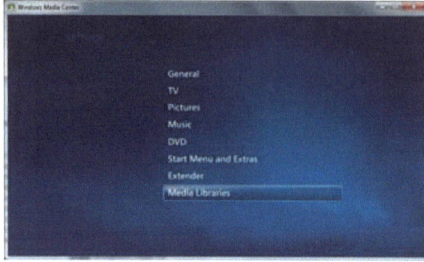

3. Then select a media library to manage. In this example, we'll be using the Videos Library

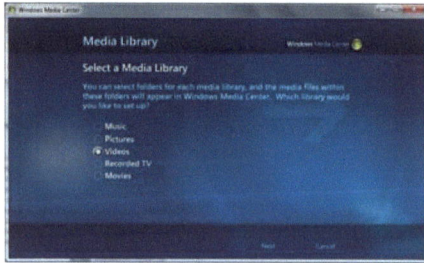

The other way is to use the remote to navigate to the media that you want to add. In this case, since we want to add to the Videos Library:

1. Using the remote, navigate to the Pictures & Videos menu and select the Videos Library.

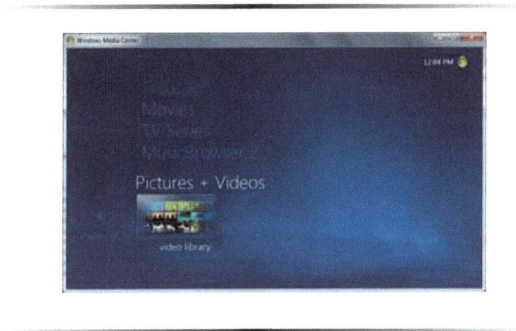

2. Once inside the Videos Library, use the 'Info' or 'i' button on your remote to bring up a small menu (you can also do this by right clicking on your mouse).

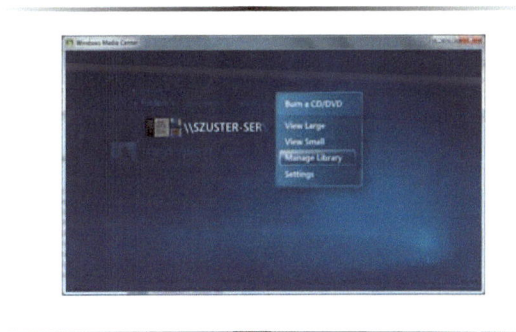

3. Choose 'Manage Library' from the menu.

171

Now that you have entered the media library configuration area, we can start the process of adding a folder:

1.   Select 'Add folders to library' and then click Next.

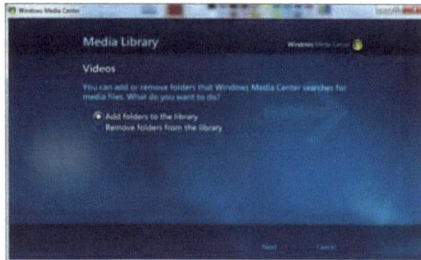

2.   Then choose 'On this Computer'. If you are adding a network share, then choose the appropriate alternative – usually 'On Another Computer'.

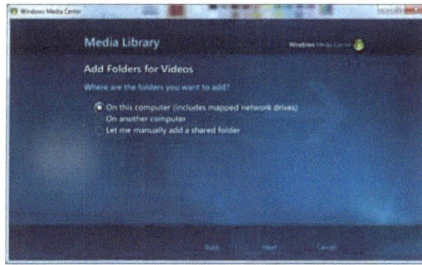

3.   Now comes the tricky part. Using your remote, navigate to 'My Videos'. This will be located under the user name, in this example ASENT.

- To expand a folder, use the remote to highlight the + and then press OK on your remote.

- To select a folder, highlight the vacant square and press OK on your remote. This will place a tick in the box to confirm your selection.

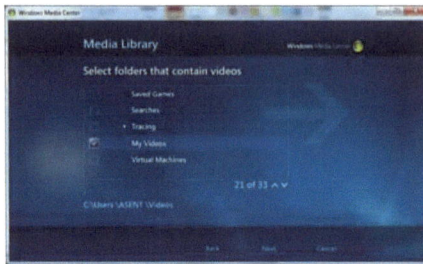

4. Once you have chosen the folder(s) you want to add, navigate to the Next button and click OK on your remote.

5. You will then be asked to verify your changes.

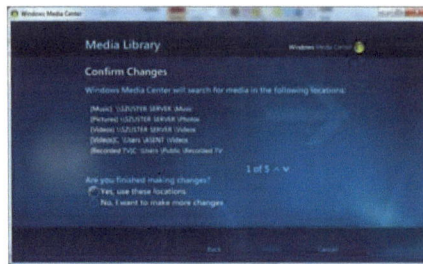

6. If you are happy, then select 'Yes, use these locations', and navigate to the Finish button and click OK on your remote.

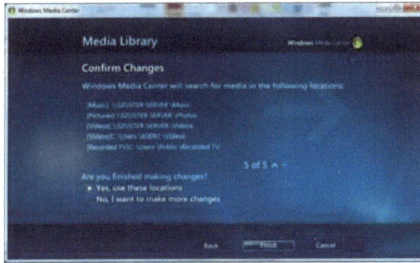

That's it! The Media Centre will then scan the folder(s) you have selected, and add the appropriate media to the library. Depending on the size of your library, this can take some time.

You then repeat this process for all the media libraries. Remember that in this context, the 'Movies' folder will be the one you created called 'DVDs'.

You will now have a fully functional Media Centre that will show Live TV, playback movies, videos, music, and will show your picture collections.

Not surprisingly, the process of removing a folder from any media library is exactly the same, with one exception: In Step 1, you select 'Remove folder from library'.

Now, this is quite a basic, Plane Jane, media centre. You will most likely want to dress it up a little, make it prettier, and add some extra functionality to it. We'll do this in Part 4 – Plugins. In the meantime, investigate your new Media Centre. See what you can do, explore and have some fun. While you are doing that, we'll look at setting up XBMC ...

:: XBMC

For XBMC, we will focus on using the Ubuntu distribution of Linux. This will vary somewhat depending on what Linux flavour you are using, however the basic process is the same.

As with the Windows section, I will be making some basic assumptions:

1. All your hardware has been installed in the media centre (TV tuners, GPU, etc...).
2. You have installed the operating system (Linux Ubuntu).

Drivers

The first thing to do after installing your operating system is to update the drivers. As we discussed earlier, drivers are the bits of software that allow the operating system to talk to the various bits of hardware. This includes the TV tuner, the processor, and even your USB ports. This makes drivers pretty important – no driver means no access to the device!

So the first thing you need to do is to install the drivers for your hardware. Linux is pretty good with its driver installation, so it will already have some basic drivers installed, but it is best to use the drivers from the manufacturer where possible. They will be more up-to-date, product specific, and in some cases, will have more features available.

There are two sources for drivers:

1.   The installation CD

2.   The manufacturer's website

Given that Linux is not the most common operating system, you may find that some CDs do not have Linux drivers. In this case, you will need to get the drivers from the manufacturer's website. These driver are the best to get anyway, as they will be the latest, most stable (usually), and most feature-rich. The ones on the CD are older and don't always deal with some of the problems that early users have faced.

The process for installation is quite straightforward. Let's follow the process using the CD you received with your hardware:

1.   Insert CD into drive.

2.   Allow the autostart function to pop up. This will ask you if you want to run the setup file. Click the setup file to run it (if you do not have the autostart function on, then open your Home Folder, navigate to File System, then the CD-ROM folder and run the installation program there).

3. Follow the prompts from the installation program. Unless you have a specific reason for doing so, use the default settings.

4. At the end of a driver installation (which can take several minutes), you may be asked to restart your computer. I usually wait until I have installed all my drivers before I do the restart.

The order that you do the driver install is not very important, however there are some things you will need drivers for before you can do much else. The obvious example is the Network Interface Card (NIC for short). This is the bit that connects you to a network and then for the internet.

So here is an order of driver installation that I recommend:

1. Motherboard drivers (also known as chipset drivers). You don't have to install the other additional software on their installation CD. In fact, I would recommend that you don't unless you know what you are doing.

   Generally, they are designed for people who over-clock their machines – something we will not be doing. The motherboard driver will cover RAM, CPU, USB, the network card, and anything else that is part of the motherboard. This can include the embedded graphics, if present.

2. Graphics driver. If you are using an Nvidia or ATI-Radeon graphics card, then download the latest drivers from their

websites. They both have a 'detect and install' plugin that will automatically determine what hardware you have and which is the best driver for it. If you have an embedded graphics chip, then you have already installed a driver in Step 1. It is still worth checking with the embedded graphics manufacturer's website for the latest driver.

3. Any other cards you might be using. This can include audio cards, USB hubs, and so on.

4. The IR receiver. Whatever IR or RF receiver you are going to use, you will need to install it so that the media centre can be controlled by your remote. Since most remotes use the Windows MCE Remote format (RC6), you will need to install the Lirc (Linux Infra-red Remote Controller) drivers. Do this by doing the following:

   1. Open Ubuntu Software Centre.
   2. Search for 'Lirc'.
   3. Install 'Infra-red Remote Control Support'.

5. The TV tuners. If you have not yet done so, install the TV tuner drivers. Usually the ones on the CD are adequate – TV tuner drivers are not often updated. Be wary of their third party TV recorders. You don't want to install these as you won't be using them, and they will slow your system down unnecessarily.

Then, restart your media centre to make sure it all works.

Ubuntu Updates

Now that we have set up Ubuntu, we need to run any updates before we start setting up XBMC. To do this:

1.   Click on the Dash Home button and type in 'update manager'.

2.   Click on the Update Manager (it will be the first item listed). The Update Manager will open.

3.　　Click on the Install Updates button to install the updates. You will be asked for your Ubuntu master password (the one you log in with).

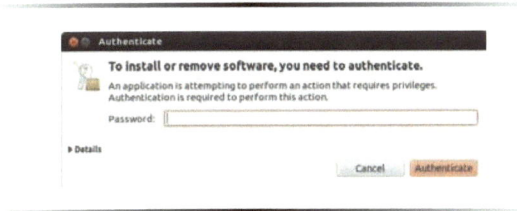

4.　　Update Manager will then start the process of installing the updates.

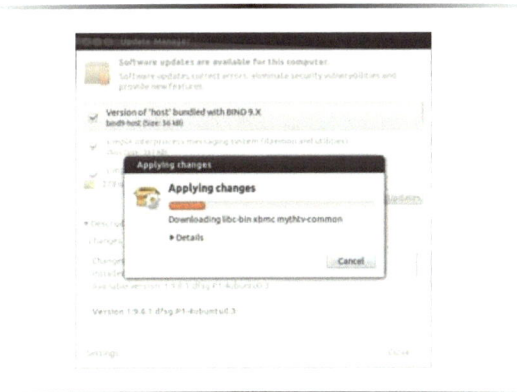

This can take some time depending on how many updates there are. We will only need to do this once, just to make sure the operating system is up-to-date before we install XBMC. There is no need to do this process on a regular basis unless:

1.　　You plan to use your Media Centre to surf the web.

2.   You use your Media Centre for other activities like emailing, gaming, etc...

Codecs

This is one of the best reasons to use Linux and XBMC: all the main codecs that you will ever use are included in the basic installation. There is no need to install a codec pack – everything is already there.

That was easy!

If you must know why we don't have to install codecs, it is because Linux (Ubuntu in particular) comes pre-installed with VLC player. VLC Player is a great media player (but not a media centre). More importantly, it comes bundled with all the codecs, so you don't have to install any!

Setting Up XBMC

Now that the system is in its 'vanilla' state, we can install XBMC. You can do this by opening the Ubuntu Software Centre and searching for XBMC. It will be the first item that comes up.

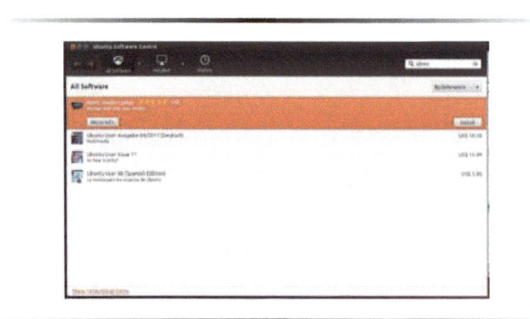

Click the install button and let it do its thing. As per normal, you will be required to enter your password to authenticate the install. However, this version will not give you live TV.

STOP!!

If you want PVR functionality (being able to watch and record live TV), then you need to get a slightly different version of XBMC and compile it. Relax ... there is a script that automates the process.

A quick note: As of printing date the next version of XBMC will have PVR functionality built it. It is in the beta versions – however version 11 (on which this book is written) does not have PVR or Live TV functionality built in, hence this process:

Download the script here: http://packages.pulse-eight.net/

I suggest you save the script to the Downloads folder.

To run the script you need to:

1.   Open a bash terminal by going to the Dash Home and typing in 'term'.

2.   The terminal will be the first option. Click on this to open the terminal window.

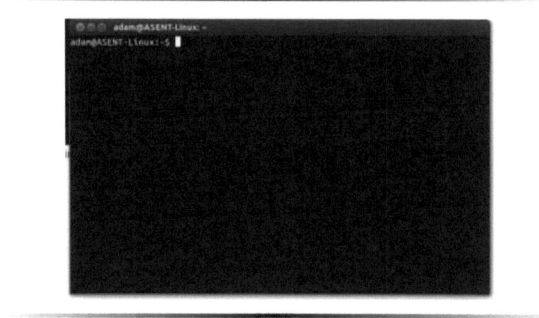

3.   Navigate to the downloads folder by typing " cd Downloads" - without the quotes - and pressing enter. Remember the capital D in Downloads – the Ubuntu file system is case sensitive.

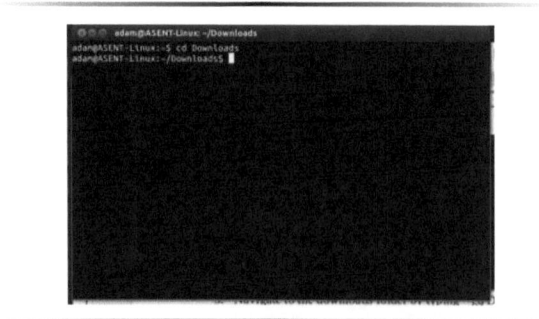

4.   Type in "chmod a+x install-xbmc.sh" - without the quotes - and press Enter.

5.   Now type "./install-xbmc.sh" - without the quotes – and press Enter.

6.   You will be asked for your master password (the one you log in to Ubuntu with). Type it in and press Enter.

7.   The installation will now commence.

8.   Once complete, type "Exit" - without the quotes - and press Enter to exit the bash terminal.

And that is the XBMC installation completed :)

Now we are ready to start the Media Centre.

Starting XBMC for the First Time

To start XBMC, you will need to click on the Dash Home icon and type in XBMC. This will show the XBMC icon which you can click to start the Media Centre.

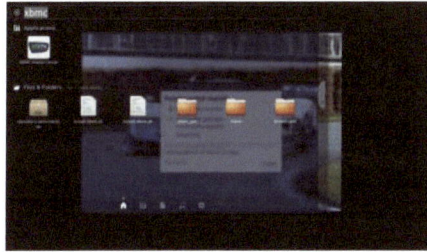

But before you start XBMC, let's quickly click and drag the XBMC icon to the launcher so it is easily available when you want it.

Now that you have added XBMC to the launcher start it up!

Setting Up the XBMC Libraries

By default, the XBMC is ready to play virtually any content you can think of. But it needs to know where the content is – and this is the first thing we need to do. I will go through the process of setting up the Video content. It is a process you can then repeat for Music and Pictures.

1. Navigate across to the Video menu and then down to the Files. Click on Files.

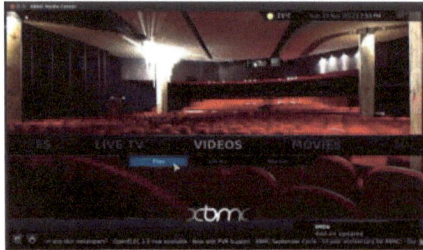

2. Select 'Add Videos...'.

3.   In the dialogue box that appears, navigate to the 'Browse…' button and select.

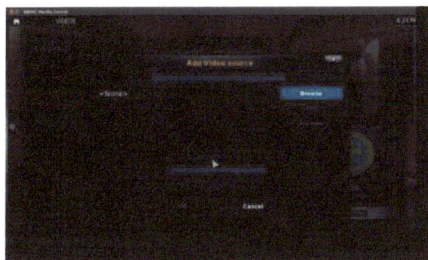

4.   You can now browse the file system and connected networks to locate your media. In this example, I have highlighted 'Windows SMB' network connection, because I have my media stored on a Windows Home Server.

A word on media folders. I strongly recommend that you install two hard drives – one for the media centre, the other for your media. The media drive should be as large as possible – at least 1Tb. On the media drive, I recommend you create at least five folders:

1.   Videos

2.   Music

3.   Pictures

4.   DVDs

5.   Recorded TV

You can then put your various media files in the appropriate folder. This will make it easy to manage your collection of media as it grows. And it will grow!

5.   Once you have selected the folder that houses your media, you will need to give it a name. Once named, click OK and you are done.

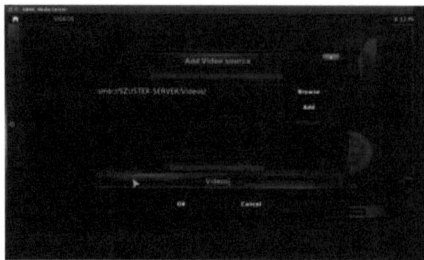

6.   Now set the 'Scrapper' for that location. A scrapper is a little app that 'scrapes' the web for information on the media files in your

folder. Since we are doing a Videos folder, I have set the scrapper as specific to movies.

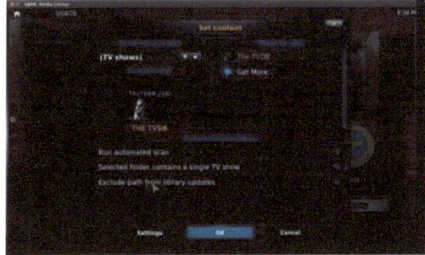

7.   The scrapper will match the background imagery to match the movie that is highlighted.

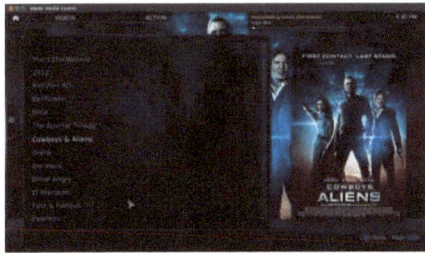

Repeat this process for Music and Photos. The only difference with Music and Pictures is that you don't select a scrapper. You can scrap the music files, but we'll cover that in Part 4 – Plugins and Apps.

Setting Up Live TV

The one thing that XBMC is missing in its default

installation is Live TV. But fear not! It is a quite straight forward thing to do.

We need to install some software so that XBMC can access the TV tuners. There are three that you can choose from:

HTS Tvheadend

Myth TV

VDR

In this book, I will focus on HTS Tvheadend, as it is easy to install and set up. It also has a small memory footprint and is accessible from any web browser. The others are OK and will work, but they are more fiddly to setup.

:: HTS Tvheadend

Installing a 'non-approved' application in Ubuntu is a bit of pain. There is a process you need to go through that involves using a bash terminal to enter in some commands that will enable us to install HTS Tvheadend. It's not too difficult, and I have created a step-by-step process for you to follow.

Before we can install the HTS Tvheadend we need to let Ubuntu know where to access the installation files. We do this by setting up a Personal Package Archive (PPA).

1. Open a bash terminal by typing "term" in the Dash Home search bar. Select Terminal to open the terminal.

2.　Type "sudo add-apt-repository ppa:adamsutton/tvheadend" - without the quotes - and press Enter.

3.　You will be asked for your masterpassword – that's the one you log in to Ubuntu with.

- The contents of Personal Package Archives are not checked or monitored. You install software from them at your own risk.

- Your system will now fetch the PPA's key. This enables your Ubuntu system to verify that the packages in the PPA have not been interfered with since they were built.

4. Now, as a one-off, you should tell your system to pull down the latest list of software from each archive it knows about, including the PPA you just added: type "sudo apt-get update" and press Enter. You will be asked for your master password again.

5. Now we can install HTS Tvheadend. Type "sudo apt-get install tvheadend" - without the quotes - and press Enter. You will again be asked for your master password.

6. You will be asked to confirm the installation. Type "y" and press Enter to continue.

7. HTS Tvheadend will now be installed. Once installation is complete, you will be asked to enter a user name for Tvheadend. Use something simple like your name.

8. Once you have entered a user name, use the down arrow on your keyboard to choose <OK> and then press Enter.

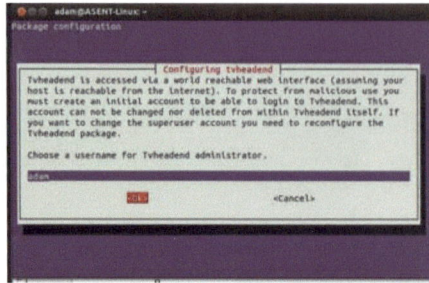

9.   Next, type in a password, then use the down
      arrow, select <OK> and press Enter.

10.   HTS   Tvheadend   is   now   ready   for
      configuration – the next screen tells you
      what the address of the configuration
      screen is. We will type this into a web
      browser shortly.

11. Press Enter to continue the installation.

12. Type "exit" and press Enter to close the bash terminal.

Now we are ready to set up and configure HTS Tvheadend:

1.   Open the HTS Tvheadend configuration
        screen by:

        •   Opening your web browser.

        •   Type "localhost:9981" - without the
                quotes - in the URL address bar and press
                Enter. This will load the HTS Tvheadend
                configuration screen.

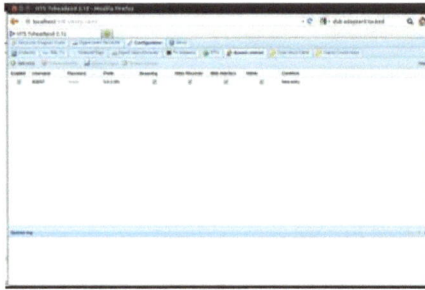

2.   Select the 'Configuration' and then 'TV
        Adapters' tab.

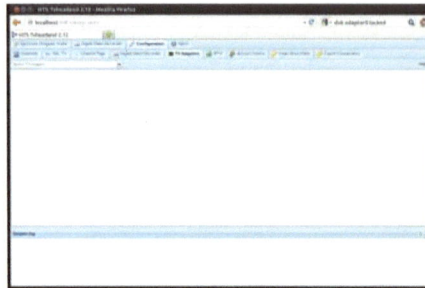

3.   From the drop-down box, select your TV tuner(s). If no tuner is listed, check that they are installed, that the drivers are installed, and that they are Linux compatible.

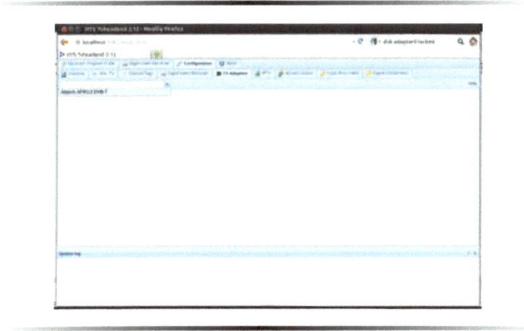

4.   In the 'General' tab, click on the 'Add DVB Network by location' button.

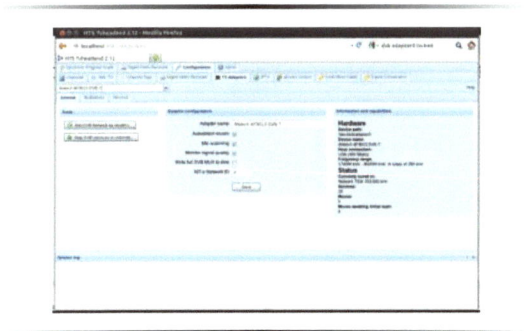

5.   Double click your country to list all the available regions. The regions are based on the TV antennae locales.

6.   Select the most appropriate locale for you.

7.   Click the 'Add DVB network' button.

8.   Next, click on the 'Services' tab to check that all your TV stations are listed.

9. Click on the 'Digital Video Recorder' tab to set the location of where the recorded TV will be stored.

10. Enter the location where your recorded TV will be stored in the section titled 'Recording System Path'.

A word on media folders. I strongly recommend that you install two hard drives – one for the media centre, the other for your media. The media drive should be as large as possible – at least 1Tb. On the media drive, I recommend you create at least five folders:

1. Videos

2. Music

3. Pictures

4. DVDs

5. Recorded TV

You can then put your various media files in the appropriate folder. This will make it easy to manage your collection of media as it grows. And it will grow!

11. Finally we need to set access permissions Click on the 'Access Control' tab.

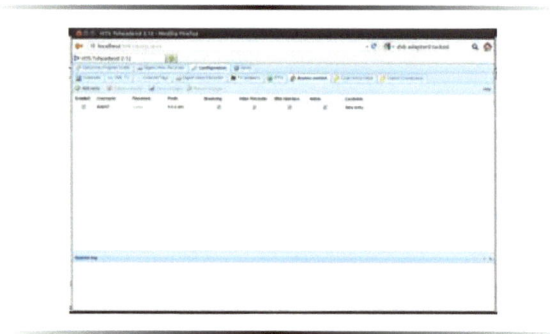

12. Click on the 'Add Entry' button.

13. Add a username and password (which you will need in XBMC) by double clicking on each, and entering the name and password you want. Make it simple – something easy to remember, unless you are planning on sharing the media centre with other users.

14.   Make sure all check-boxes are ticked.

15.   Click the 'Save Changes' button.

And that's it. You can now close the HTS Tvheadend window in your browser.

The last part of setting up live TV is the Live TV settings in XBMC itself. This basically involves ensuring XBMC is set up to access the HTS Tvheadend software:

1.   Open XBMC.

2.   Go to the 'System' tab and open it.

3.   Select the 'Add-ons' menu and open it.

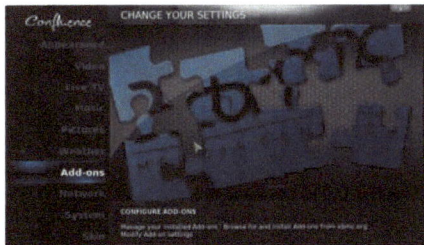

4.   Select the 'Installed Add-ons' menu and open it.

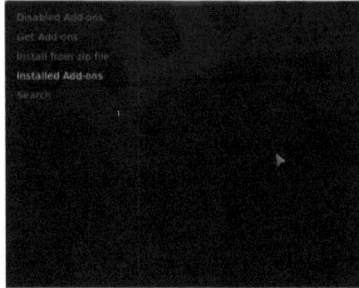

5.   Go to the 'PVR Clients' menu and open.

6.   Go to 'Tvheadend HTSP Client' and enter it.

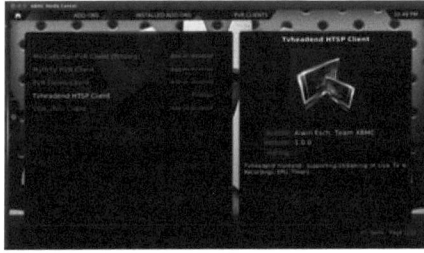

7.   If not already done, click the enable button.

8.   Select 'Configure'.

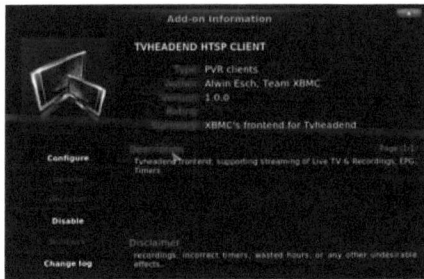

9.   Set the username and password that you created during the HTS Tvheadend configuration.

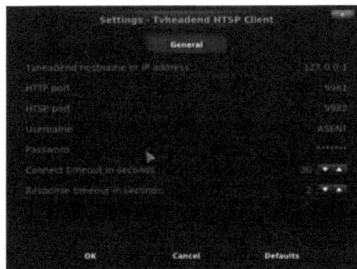

10. Click 'OK' to save.

11. Close the 'Add-on Information' window.

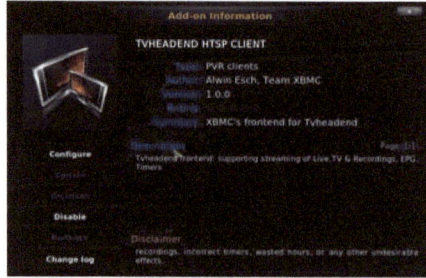

12. Click on the Home button at the top left of the screen.

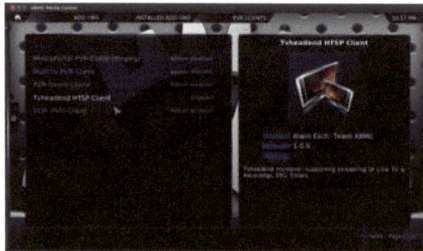

13. Select 'Live TV' and enter.

14.   Select a TV channel and ENJOY!

So there you have it – you have now set up Live TV
through XBMC! XBMC is now a perfect media centre that
will play everything you can throw at it, plus record and
watch live TV.

Part 4

:: Media Centre Plugins

Now that we have a working media centre, you're happy right? Well, we can do more with our media centre through the use of plugins. Plugins are little apps that extend or enhance the media centre. There are a range of them available for both Windows Media Centre and XBMC.

Windows Media Centre is not so user-friendly when it comes to plugins. The WMC community has been quite busy however, given that there is no 'official' support for plugins in WMC, and the installation process is a little more difficult, usually requiring a mouse and keyboard.

The XBMC community has also been quite productive with its plugins. Not only that, it has a built-in plugin centre that enables you to easily find and install plugins for a wide variety of activities. Simply use your remote, locate and install – it's that easy!

In Part 4, we will explore plugins for both Windows Media Centre and XBMC. We will look at which ones you should have, which ones you might like, and where you can find them. We will also cover the installation process for both Media Centre software packages.

For those of you who are using Plex, the process for XBMC will apply to you. The biggest difference between XBMC and Plex is the sheer number of plugins available – XMBC has a lot more to play with. Plex users will also find that some plugins that work for XBMC may work with Plex (but not normally the other way around).

So, let's get into it!

:: Windows Media Centre

For all their ease of use and intuitive user interface, plugins are a major weakness for Windows Media Centre. Microsoft do not officially support plugins, nor do they supply a method of installation. All of this means that you will need a keyboard and mouse to install your plugins.

There are some excellent plugins for WMC. What follows is a collection of the best. We'll discuss what they are for and how to install them.

My Channel Logos

The first must-have WMC plugin is My Channel Logos. As the name suggests, it is a plugin that adds channel logos to your TV guide turning it from this:

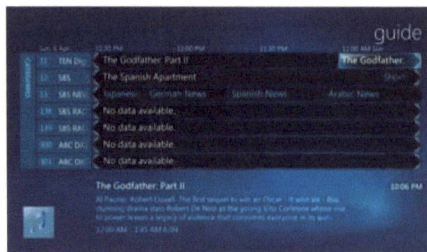

into this:

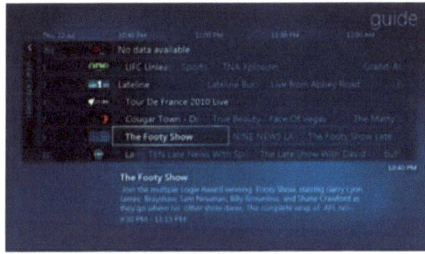

The change is small, but significant. Not only does it provide a bit more colour to your TV guide screen, but it makes the whole TV/PVR experience more polished, and it will impress the heck out of your friends! It also makes it a lot easier to navigate – particularly for older people and those who are a little techno-phobic.

First things first: download it here http://www.mychannellogos. com

I highly recommend spending $5 for the full version if you can. It helps the developers maintain and improve the plugin, but more importantly, it allows you to automatically populate the guide logos where possible. Auto-population is correct about 98% of the time. For the other 2%, you will have to add the logos manually.

Auto-population will save you a lot of time by eliminating a boring and repetitive task.

The first time you run My Channel Logos, it will connect to the web and download all the channels it thinks it needs. This won't take too long, assuming that you have ADSL or similar broadband, maybe 60 seconds.

It is possible that not every logo will be automatically added. This is normally due to My Channel Logos not having a logo for that specific channel. So where do you get a logo from? The answer is Wikipedia.

To find a logo:

1.   Open Google and search for the TV station name, ie, GEM.

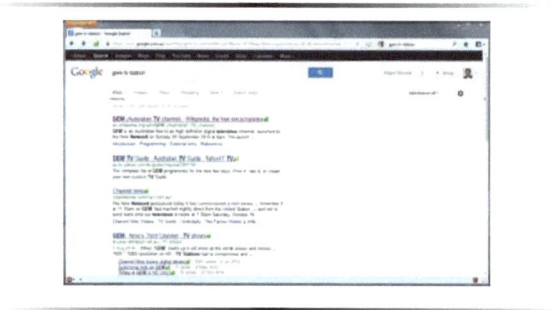

2.   Look through the search results for a Wikipedia entry. Click on the link.

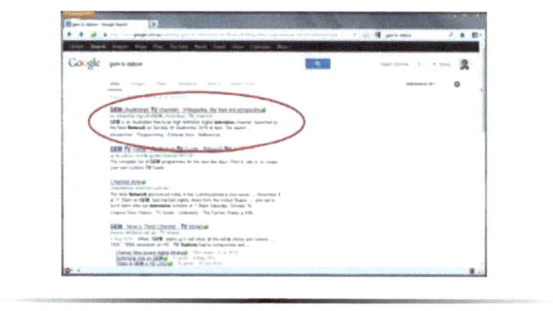

3.   Make sure the Wikipedia entry is the correct TV channel for your country.

4. On the right-hand side of the Wikipedia entry is a fast facts column, on top of which will be the logo you are looking for.

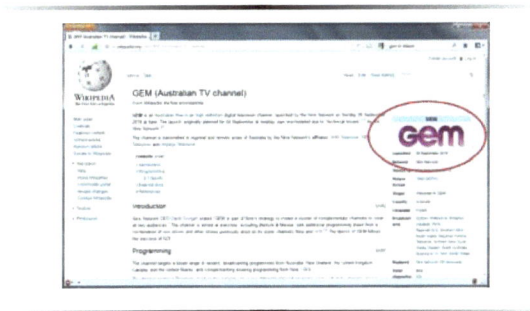

5. Right click on the logo and select 'Save Picture As ...'. Remember where you save it! It will be saved as a png file format which is exactly what we want (it will have a clear background).

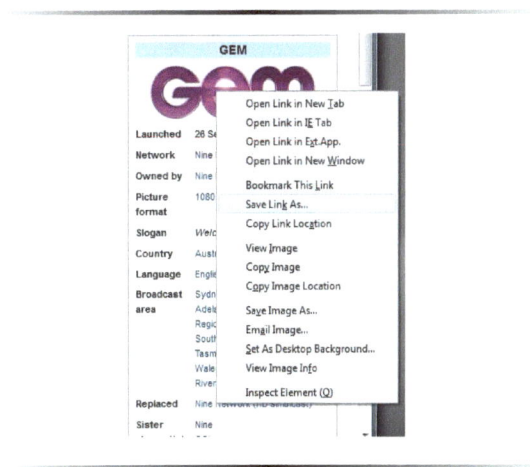

Now that you have downloaded the logo, we need to tell My Channel Logos where it is:

1.   Open My Channel Logos (click the start button on the desktop and type in 'My channel').

2.   In the column titled 'channel without logos', select the channel in question.

3.   On the right-hand side of the window, there is a black strip which has the channel number, a blue 'add logo' box, and the channel name. Click on the 'add logo' box.

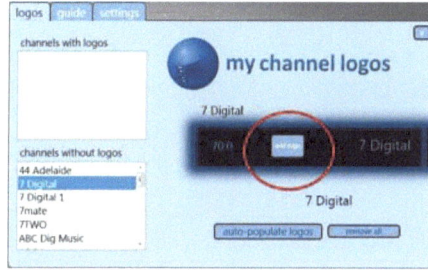

4.   A windows dialogue box will open. Navigate
      to the location where you saved the logo a
      little earlier (you do remember, don't you?
      and open it.

My Channel Logo will add the logo to the station and
move it up to the column titled 'channels with logos'.

You will need to do this process for each un-assigned TV
station. This is where spending $5 saves a whole lot of
time!

Now open your Windows Media Centre and check out
the TV guide - awesome!

Total Media Theatre

Not a plugin exactly, Total Media Theatre is only required if you are going to be watching Blu-ray discs. As mentioned earlier, neither Windows nor Linux offer native Blu-ray playback, so each system requires an add-on.

In Windows Media Centre, there are two options:

1. Total Media Theatre.
2. Power DVD.

These programs work by providing a WMC interface that:

1. Minimises WMC.
2. Opens the program (TMT5 or PDVD) in an interface that looks like WMC.
3. Plays the BD in this WMC look-a-like interface.
4. Exits and returns to WMC when you exit out of the look-a-like interface.

It sounds complicated, but in fact you are actually using a different kind of software that looks like and operates like WMC. This is the only way to watch Blu-ray in WMC, as Microsoft will not support native Blu-ray playback, even in Windows 8.

Both these programs have plugins which enable you to use them from within the Windows Media Centre. After using both extensively, I personally find that Total Media Theatre (TMT) is the way to go. The operation is more seamless, is integrated better into the WMC experience, and offers you the ability to make setting changes using your remote.

NOTE: Both of these programs are not free. In fact they come in at around $100 each – making it quite an expensive option. If money is a problem, then I am afraid that Blu-ray playback from the Windows Media Centre may not be for you.

Both programs do offer a free trial, so you can see how it all works, however the trials run out after 15/30 days – at which point you will need to buy a serial number.

So, in this book, I am only going to refer to TMT, however the process is essentially the same for Power DVD. The location of settings that I recommend that you need to change will be in different locations, but you should still set them to what I am recommending here.

So let's get to it.

Firstly, download and purchase your copy of Total Media Theatre from their website:

http://www.arcsoft.com/totalmedia-theatre/

Once it is downloaded, run the installer, as you would any other program. You will need to restart your media centre to complete the installation.

You will most likely be asked to install an update. Please do so. Updates for Blu-ray are fairly regular as the encryption used is changed several times a year. The updates allow you to play the newest Blu-ray discs.

Once we have performed any updates, we need to change some specific settings:

1. Open Windows Media Centre.

2. Navigate to the Total Media Centre 5 menu in the Windows Media Centre.

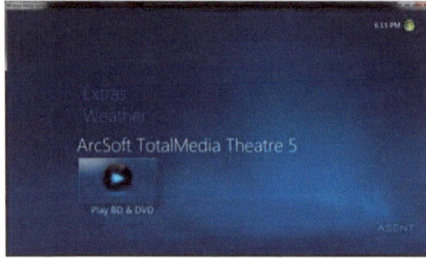

3.   Select the setting menu and click OK.

4.   Go into the Playback menu.

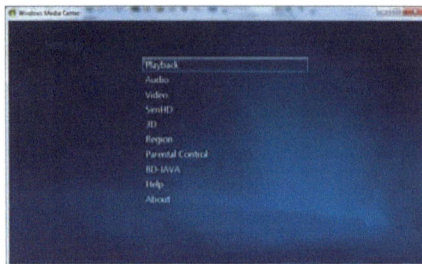

5.   Tick the "Auto Refresh Rate" box and change the "Auto-resume" option to 'Resume from last position'. Do this by navigating to the + and – signs next to the option and clicking OK on your remote. This will scroll through the available options. Navigate to the Save button at the top left of the screen and OK to save and exit the Playback settings menu.

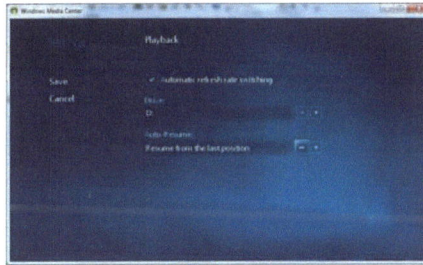

6.   Navigate to the BD-Java menu and enter.

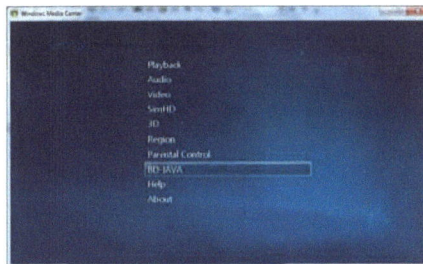

7.   Change the "Allow Access to Internet Certification" option to 'Always approve every disc'. This assumes that you have a constant connection to the internet via your LAN connection to your media centre You do have a LAN connection, don't you? (this option will work with wireless, but as mentioned several times before – you shouldn't be using wireless).

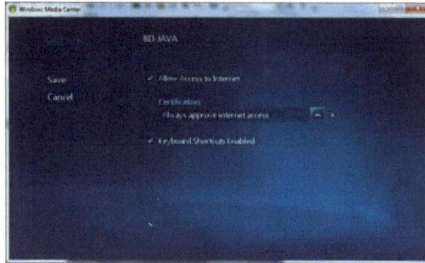

8.   Then move to the Save button at the top left and click OK to save and exit.

9.   Navigate to the Audio Settings menu.

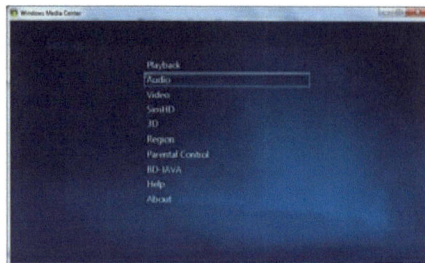

10.   Check that your sound card is selected. This may not always be the case. If you are not using a sound card – ie, you are running your audio through HDMI, then make sure your graphics card is selected, ie, AMD High Definition Audio Device.

11.   Make sure the Speaker Output is appropriate. Again, if using HDMI, then it should be HDMI; if using optical then S/PDIF; etc...

12.   Set Mixing Mode to 'Smart Mixing'. This will output either Dolby or DTS depending on what format is used by the Blu-ray disc.

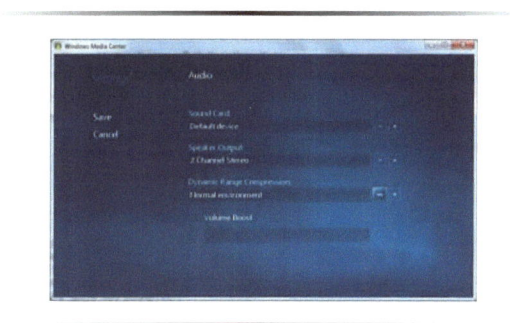

And that's it. None of the other settings should need to be touched, but by all means, play with them if you like.

The only catch with running TMT5 (or Power DVD) is that when you play a DVD, Windows Media Centre will ask you which program you want to play it with:

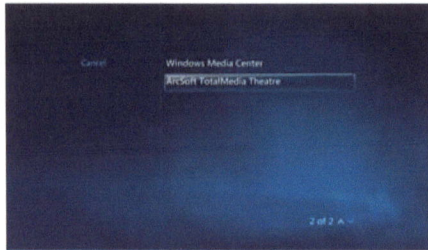

I recommend that you choose Windows Media Centre when you play your DVDs.

This all depends on if you have autoplay enabled on your media centre in Windows. If you don't then you will not be asked – you can simply navigate to the Movies > Play DVD icon to start playback.

The last thing we want to do is to clean the Windows Media Start menu by removing the Arcsoft Total Media Theatre5 icon.

1.   Navigate to Tasks > Settings on the Start menu.

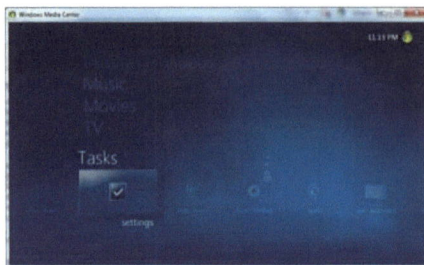

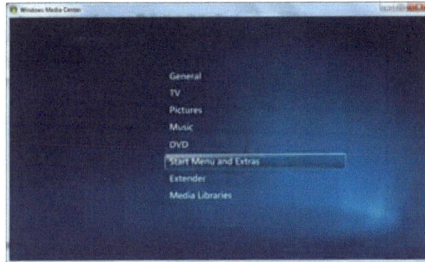

2.   Go into the Start menu and Extras menu.

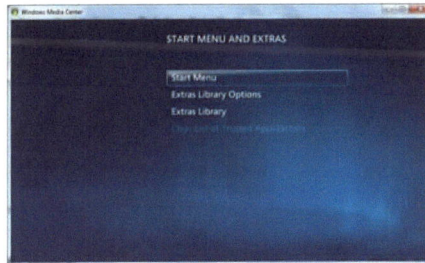

3.   Select the Start menu option.

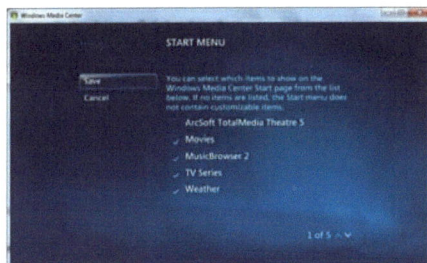

4.   Untick 'Arcsoft Total Media Theatre 5' and then save your changes.

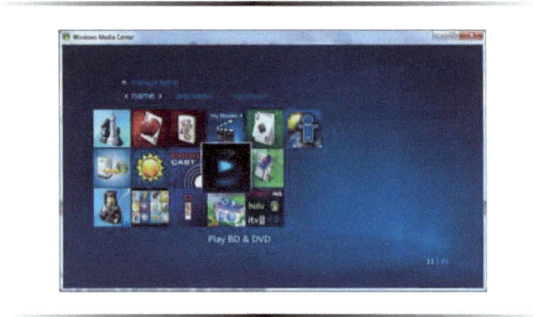

5.   Exit back to the Start menu.

You will now no longer see the Arcsoft Total Media Theatre 5 icon in the start menu, however you can still use your remote to access it from the Extras Library in the Extras menu:

When you insert a Blu-ray disc, Total Media Theatre will start automatically.

Region Free DVD/BD

Have you ever had one of those DVDs that just won't play in your DVD player? Then when you check the back of the DVD cover you find out it is from another region? Well, there are two plugins that will overcome this problem.

But how did the problem come about?

In order to reduce piracy, movie companies decided to

divide DVDs and Blu-rays into global regions so that copies made in one region wouldn't work in another. This means that the illegal copies that are made in Asia won't play in Australia or Europe.

There are actually 10 DVD regions and 3 Blu-ray ones:

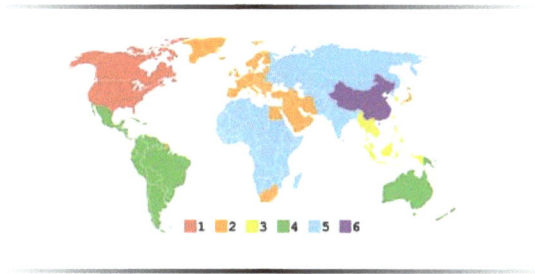

Code	DVD Regions
0	All Regions
1	North America
2	Europe, Middle East, Greenland & South Africa
3	SE Asia
4	South America, Australia & NZ
5	Africa, Russia & rest of Asia
6	China
7	unused
8	International Venues (planes, boats, etc...)
All	All regions

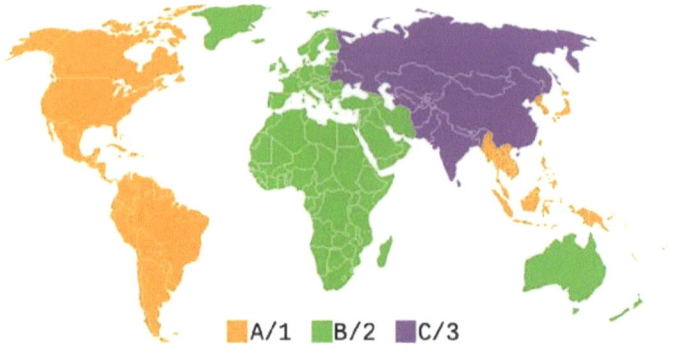

Code	Bluray Region
A	North America, South America & SE Asia
B	Africa, Europe, Greenland, Australia & NZ
C	Russia, China, India & rest of Asia

This makes it very annoying for those people in Australia who buy legitimate DVDs from America, as they simply won't play. Now, you can change your DVD/Blu-ray player region code to play those discs, but you can only do it 4 times before the player is locked - permanently!

The solution is software. Let's talk about the two best options:

> AnyDVD/HD
>
> DVD43

Both these programs enable you to play any DVD from any region around the world on your media centre. But AnyDVD/HD takes it a step further by enabling you to do the same with Blu-ray discs as well.

:: Any DVD

AnyDVD is the best option. This program removes all forms of DVD and Blu-ray protection, meaning that your media centre can play any disc from anywhere in the world. It is also updated frequently which is important for Blu-ray discs as the copy protection changes on a regular basis. This means all the newest movies can be played, hassle-free.

The downside is money. AnyDVD is a commercial product and it does cost money. But if you watch Blu-ray discs, it is a wise investment, and money well spent.

You can download the free AnyDVD trial from here: http://www.slysoft.com/en/

Run the installation file to install. You will need to reboot your media centre to complete the installation.

AnyDVD runs in the background and scans any optical disc that is inserted, removing the protection as required. You don't have to do anything!

There are a range of options you can use to tweak AnyDVD but you don't really need to as the default options are fine.

:: DVD43

DVD43 does exactly what the name suggests. It enables you to play a DVD from any region on your media centre - and it does this for free!

The downside to DVD43 is that it is not being developed anymore. Not that it needs to be for DVDs. Neither will it work with Blu-ray discs. But if you only watch DVDs and have a collection that you purchased on your last overseas holiday – DVD43 is perfect. And free :)

You can download DVD43 here: http://www.dvd43.com/

Simply run the downloaded installation file. DVD43 will then run in the background scanning discs when you insert them into your media centre.

Big Screen Weather

What's the weather like outside? Well, now you can use your media centre to find out. There are quite a few weather apps available for WMC, however the best, especially for Australians, is Big Screen Weather 2.

You can download it here: http://bigscreenglobal.com

You can try it out free for 30 days and if you like it, it only costs $20.

To install Big Screen Weather, simply download it and install. Follow the prompts to complete a standard installation.

Once you have installed the plugin, you will need to activate it. This is required for the 30-day trial too – you will be issued with a serial number which you will need to complete the registration process:

1.   Open the Start menu.

2.   Click on All Programs.

3.   Navigate to the Big Screen folder and select the 'Product Registration' program.

4.   When prompted, paste the serial number (either the trial or full version) and click next.

5.   That's it!

And now we are ready to use it:

1.   To access Big Screen Weather, navigate to the Extras Library and select the icon with the sun in it.

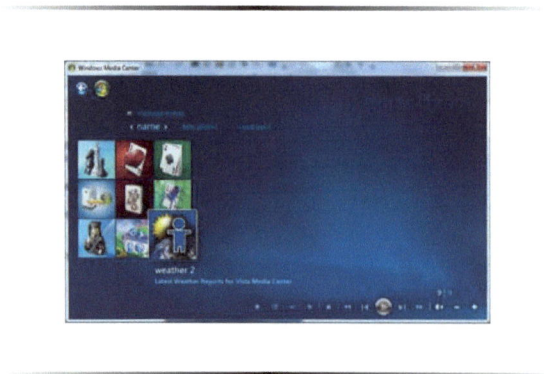

2.   The first time you run the plugin, you will be asked which language you want to use.

3.   Then you will need to select your continent.

4.   Then your country ...

5.   Depending on which country you choose, you may also be asked which state/province you are in.

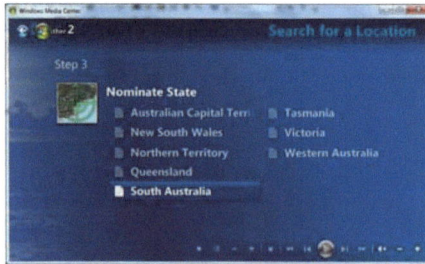

6.   And finally, choose your weather observation location.

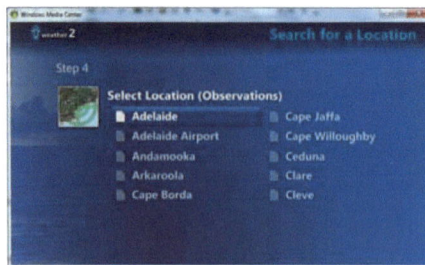

You now have a fully functional, and very useful, weather forecaster on your media centre!

With this plugin, you can set various locations to watch – which is particularly useful if you travel frequently. There are also radar maps for you to view, current weather observations, and extended 7-day forecasts.

mcShoutcast

One of the great things about a media centre is that you can stream internet radio. This gives you access to hundreds, if not thousands, of radio stations from around the globe. Looking for Egyptian Hip-hop Reggae? It's probably available on an internet radio station somewhere!

In order to access these internet radio stations, we will need a plugin called mcShoutcast. Shoutcast is an internet streaming service that lists, according to their website, some 13,000 web radio stations that you can listen to. What mcShoutcast does is make all that internet radio available to your WMC.

You can get it here: http://en.mcetools.de/

You can download a free trial version – if you like it and want to use it afterwards, it will cost you $10. Money well spent in my opinion!

After downloading the plugin, install it in the usual way by running the downloaded installation file.

mcShoutcast is installed in the Music menu on your

media centre, in the Radio section. Think of mcShoutcast as a radio station.

In order to find and listen to a station, do the following:

1. Navigate to the Music menu and then Radio.

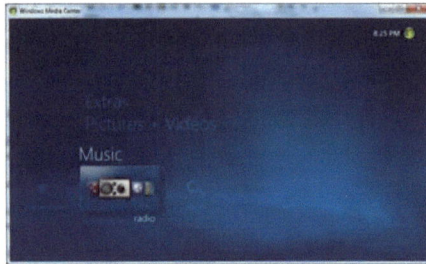

2. Then, select mcShoutcast and press OK.

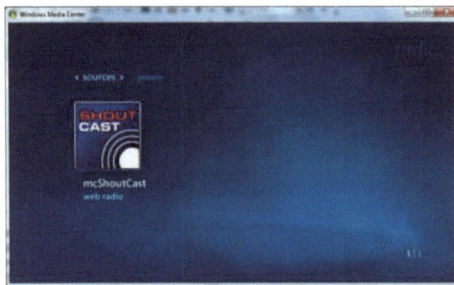

3. Once inside, you'll see an almost blank screen. Don't worry! It is showing you your favourite stations – and since you haven't added any yet, it's currently blank.

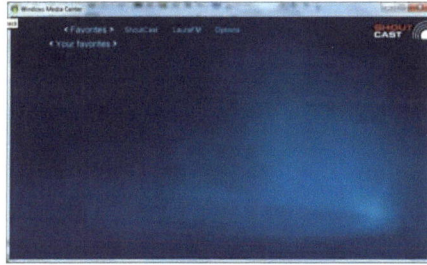

4. When you start mcShoutcast, it will download and update the web station listings and URLs. These are updated by mcShoutacast and by enthusiastic users. This can take several minutes. When it is finished, you will see something similar to this:

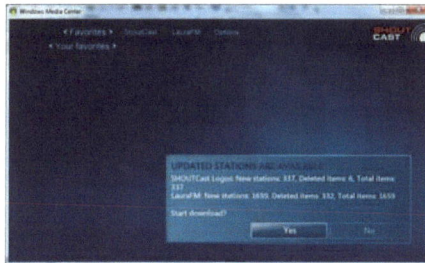

5. Once the update has completed, you can start searching for web stations. A keyboard can be handy for this, but is not essential. Navigate up and across to highlight Shoutcast. A word of warning – it is not always easy to see if a menu is highlighted. If you are not sure, move left or right – that should help identify the menu that has been selected.

6. Choose a folder! You can sort by genre, Top 500, or do a manual search (this is where a keyboard is handy). When you select a folder, you will get a menu like this that comes up. Click Open Folder to ... well you get the idea.

7. Then, select your channel and press ok to reveal the menu.

8. If you like the channel, I strongly recommend you tick 'Add to favourites', so that it will appear on the screen when you first open mcShoutcast.

9.   Then click Play to play. Simple!

You will also notice that there is a menu next to Shoutcast called 'Laura FM'. Laura FM is similar to Shoutcast, but it also categorises radio stations by location, as well as by genre. So, you might like to start your search for Egyptian Hiphop Reggae by looking in the Egyptian section ...

And there you are - access to a world of internet radio from the comfort of your couch. And all you need is your remote!

Music Browser

If you have a large music collection, then using the built-in Music sorter is a bit of a pain. You either need a keyboard to find something, or a very strong thumb to click left or right as many times as is required.

It gets even worse if your meta-data is not up to scratch. WMC sorts music by using the meta-data tags that are attached to the music files. It generally uses Artist, Album Artist, and Genre, to sort the music for you. If your music has no meta-tags (ie, you have lossless flac files), then you will not see the music in WMC.

This is where Music Browser comes in. It shows you your music collection by folder structure. Anyone with a large (even medium) size music collection can sort their music by artist, usually in the format:

Artist > Album

Large collections can even be sorted by genre and/or alphabetically. For example, my personal music collection is sorted as follows:

Genre > Alphabetical > Artist > Album

This is a far easier way to find music, in my opinion.

I also have a lot of DJ mixes which do not have meta-data – at least, nothing accurate. So, searching by folder is my only real option.

You can get Music Browser here:

http://www.musicbrowser2.com/

Once you have installed the plugin, you open it from the Windows Media Centre start menu. You will find your entire music collection sorted by folder structure. It uses the folder that Windows Media Centre has set to use for music.

The first time you open MusicBrowser2, it will scan your music collection for meta-data. If you have a large collection, this may take some time. One collection I scanned recently had over 170GB of music – it took about 10 minutes to complete this first scan.

To use music browser:

1.   Navigate the start Menu to find Music Browser 2 and select.

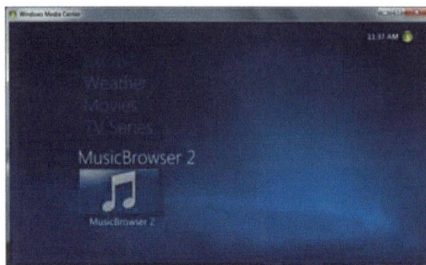

2. Navigate to the folder of music that you want to play.

3. Scroll to the top of the page until the Actions icon is highlighted.

4. Select the Actions icon and then choose Play.

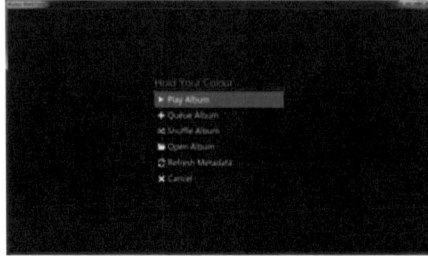

You can also play a single file in the same way.

Made 4 Media Centre

One of the biggest complaints about WMC is that there has never been a way to install plugins without dragging out the keyboard and mouse, opening your web browser, and using the '2 foot' installation process.

Made 4 Media centre changes all that, by allowing you to use the remote to select various plugins, install them, and start using them. This plugin makes WMC more like XBMC in this respect.

You can download it here: http://madeformediacenter.com

You will need to create a free account at the site in order to login and download the 'Media Centre Addin'. Install it and then:

1.   Navigate to The Extras menu and select the Made For Media Centre plugin.

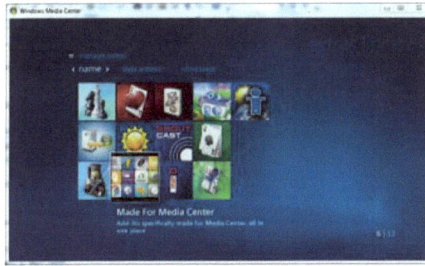

2. The first time you open Made for Media Centre, you will need to log in using the details you registered while downloading the installation file.

3. Once you are in, you can start browsing plugins.

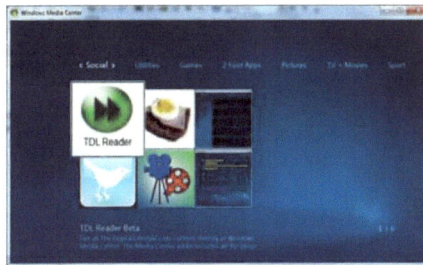

4.   When you find something interesting, select
        it to see a brief description and the install
        button. Click OK if you want to install

        Confirm your installation to proceed.

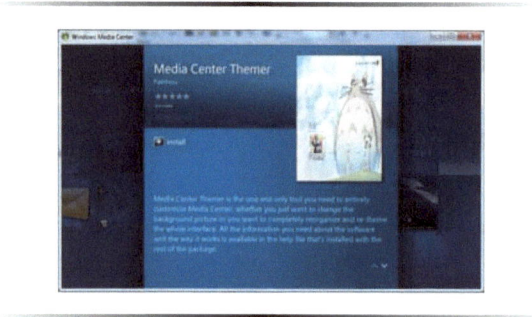

5.   Installation details are given in the final
        confirmation (that's two confirmations
        for safety!).

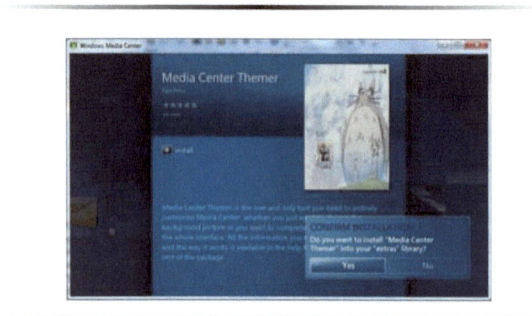

6.   You will be shown a progress bar of your
        download.

7.   Once installed, the new plugin will be available from your Extras menu.

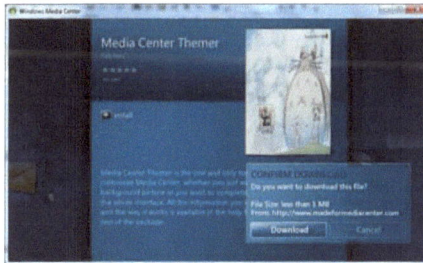

And that's it! You can explore a range of plugins for WMC right from your couch – easy as pie.

A word of warning with this plugin: Since it is integrating a lot of content from different providers, it is prone to crashing at times. When it does so, you will be returned to the Extras menu in WMC. Simply open the plugin in again to continue using it.

A final note: This plugin is really for those who want to play around with their Media Centre experience. If you are a first time user, I do not recommend using this plugin. Wait until you are comfortable with all the features and functionality of your media centre, not to mention the other plugins discussed in this book, before playing with this one.

:: XBMC

One of the best things about XBMC is its integrated plugins functionality. Built right into XBMC is the ability to surf add-ons. You can install any of these with the click of a button on your remote.

You can even search the web for extra add-ons and install those from a zip file – although you will need a mouse and keyboard to do this.

So first of all, let's look at how to install an add-on, and then we'll look at some 'must have' add-ons for your XBMC media centre.

Installing an Add-on

Installing add-ons in XBMC is very easy. This process applies to virtually all add-ons.

1.   Navigate to the 'Settings' option on the System tab and Enter.

2.   Select the Add-Ons menu and Enter it.

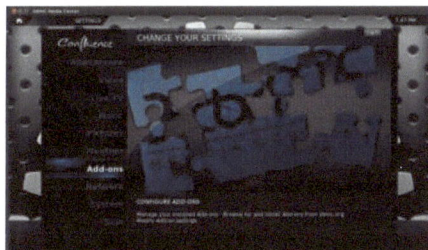

3.   To browse the add-ons available to you, choose 'Get Add-ons'.

4.   Choose your repository. XBMC.org is the default and contains add-ons that have been approved and tested by the XBMC team. A great place to start!

5.   Now you can start browsing. Choose a category to see what add-ons are available. In this example, we will check out the Weather add-ons.

6.   By navigating over an add-on, the right hand window will display information about the add-on.

7.　　When you select a specific add-on, you will be shown even more information and a menu.

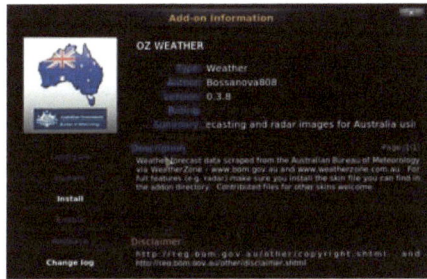

8.　　At this point, you can install the add-on by clicking/selecting 'Install'.

9.　　Once the add-on is installed, you will be returned to the add-on category, and you'll notice that the add-on is 'enabled'.

That's it! You have installed an add-on and are now using it. However, some (read most) add-ons have settings that you can configure.

Configuring an Add-on

Configuring an add-on is also quite straightforward. You may have noticed that when you installed the add-on, there was a greyed-out button labelled 'Configure'.

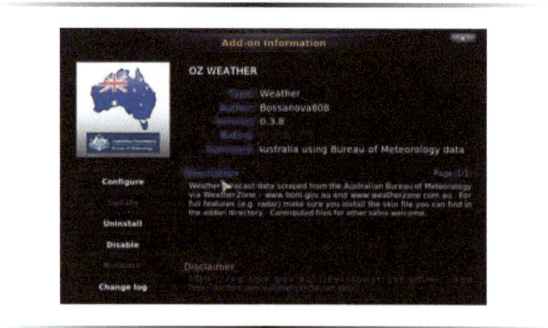

Click on the configure button to reveal the options you can change. Obviously, this will be different for each add-on, but here is a picture to give you an idea:

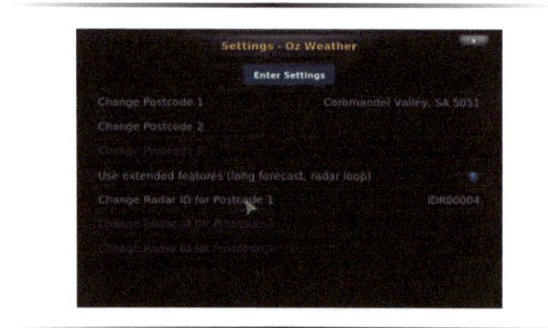

Installing Add-ons from Zip files

Now, XBMC.org is not the only place from which you can install add-ons. To find out what other add-ons are available, you can check out this page:

http://wiki.xbmc.org/index.php?title=Unofficial_add-on_repositories

or do a Google search for 'unoffical xbmc addons'.

After searching, you will find the add-on that you are looking for. Download the zip file and save it to a place you can remember (normally the default is your 'Downloads' folder).

Now it is time to install the add-on from the zip file that you have downloaded:

1.   Navigate to the 'Settings' option on the System tab and Enter.

2.   Select the Add-Ons menu and Enter it.

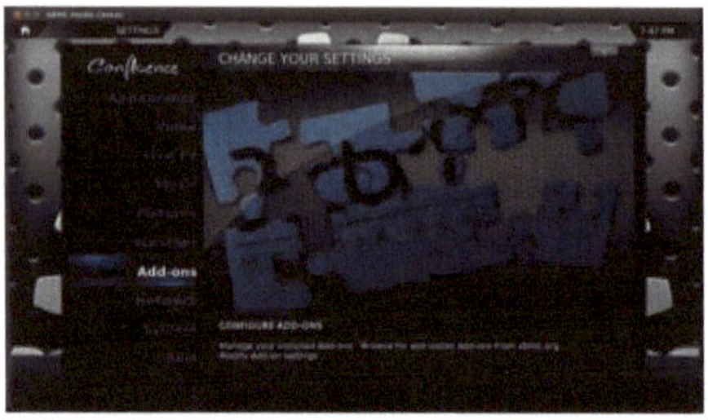

3.   This time, we will be using 'Install from zip file'.

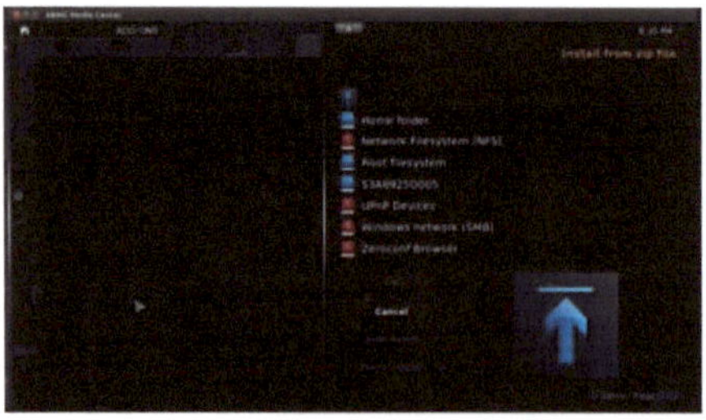

4.   A new window will appear on the right which will allow you to navigate through your folder structure to the zip file you downloaded.

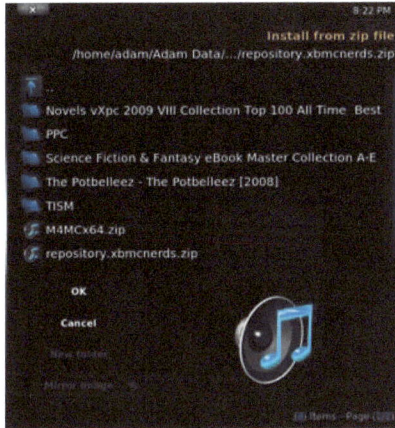

5.   Once you have found the file, select it
      and click OK.

6.   When the zip file is installed, you will be
      returned to the Add-On menu

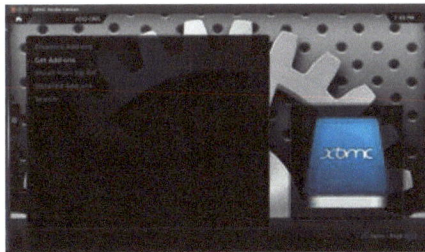

7.   Now you can go into the 'Get Add-ons'
      section and you will see the new repository
      available.

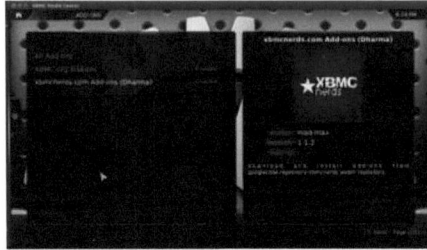

8.   From there, you follow the process outlined earlier to check out and install the new add-ons.

Now that we know how to install add-ons, let's look at some 'must have' add-ons that will make your media centre experience even more amazing!

XBMC Library Auto Update

This great add-on gives XBMC the ability to auto-update library information. By default, XBMC scans your directories once – when you add them – and then does precious little other scanning. This means that when you add new CDs or movies to your collection, XBMC will not scrape meta-data for these files.

XBMC Library Auto Update forces XBMC to update the library information on a regular basis, more like the way that Windows Media Centre does.

To install this add-on go to:

1.   Navigate to the 'Settings' option on the System tab and click.

2.   Navigate to the Add-ons menu item and
        click.

3.   Select 'Get Add-ons'.

4. Select 'XBMC.org Add-ons'.

5. Select 'Program Add-ons'.

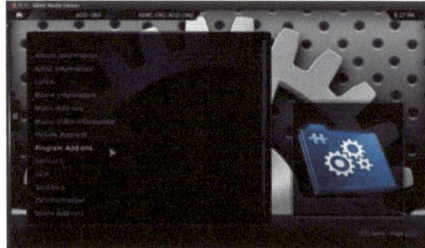

6. Scroll down until you can select 'XBMC Library Auto Update'.

254

7.   Select 'Install' to install

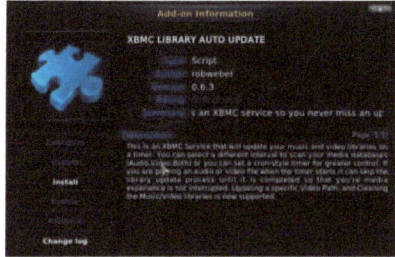

8.   Once installed, you will be returned to the Program Add-ons menu. Click the XBMC Library Auto Update add-on to configure.

9.   Select the configure button to display the configuration options.

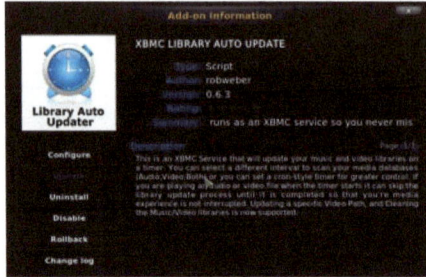

10.   From here, you can change a range of configuration options, including how frequently you want to update the libraries, and which libraries you want updated.

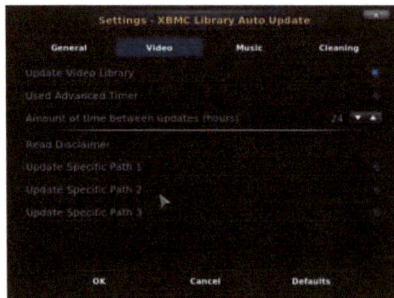

11.   The default settings are fine. Select OK to save and you are done!

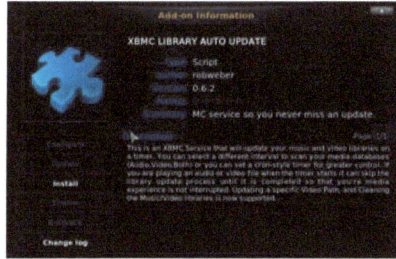

You completely control when and what gets scanned, and you can tell the software to delay scanning when you are using the media centre (watching a movie, or whatever).

MakeMKV

Unbuntu, for all its greatness, does not play Blu-ray discs natively (neither does Windows Media Centre). In order to do so, you will need to install the MakeMKV plugin.

This is a two part process:

1. Install the MakeMKV program.
2. Install the plugin.

First, is the MakeMKV program itself. Sadly, this is not available through the Ubuntu Software Centre, so we will need to compile it ourselves.

Instructions on this can be found here:

http://www.makemkv.com/forum2/viewtopic.php?f=3&t=5266

Now, if you are not familiar with command line compilation (and it can sound scary!), relax. I have a step-by-step guide to help you with this.

1. Firstly. download the following script and save it somewhere – your Downloads folder is a good place: http://dl.dropbox com/u/18055299/buildMakeMkv.sh

2. Now open the terminal by going to the Dash Home and typing in 'term'.

3. The terminal will be the first option. Click on that to open the terminal window.

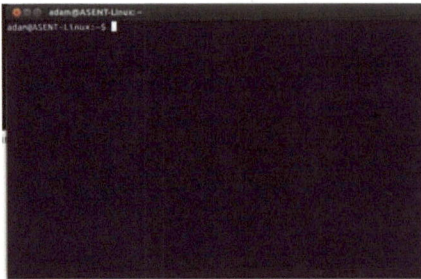

4.   Navigate to the downloads folder by typing "cd Downloads" - without the quotes - and pressing Enter. Remember the capital D in Downloads – the Ubuntu file system is case sensitive.

5.   Now type in "chmod a+x buildMakeMkv.sh" - without the quotes - and press Enter.

6.   Next, type "./buildMakeMkv.sh" - without the quotes - and press Enter.

7. You will be asked which version to download and install. Use whatever is suggested, in this case 1.7.7

8. You will also be asked for your password to authenticate installation. This is the same password you use to log in to Ubuntu.

9. The download and build will then commence. After the files have been downloaded, you will be asked if you want to continue the install. Obviously, we want to say Yes. Press Y and Enter to continue.

10. Once the software is installed (and this will take a couple of minutes), you will be asked to read, and then to agree to, the terms of the End User Licence Agreement. Press Enter to read the terms and then ...

11. ... scroll down to the bottom of the page and type "q" to exit. Then type in "yes" and press Enter to agree to the licence agreement.

12. When the install has finished, the terminal window will close itself.

And now MakeMKV is installed!

The next step is to install the plugin:

1. Download the plugin from XBMC forum: http://forum.xbmc.org/showthread php?tid=67420

2. Now install the plugin from the zip file you downloaded. We covered this process earlier in this section.

3.   And that's it!

After the add-on is installed, you will be able to configure it by going to the Video Add-ons. But there is nothing in the configuration you should need to alter. If it ain't broke, don't fix it!

To play a Blu-ray disc:

1.   Go to the Add-ons item in the Video menu.

2.   Select the 'Bluray Player with MakeMKV' add-on and press Enter.

3.   Then insert your Blu-ray disc and choose 'Play   Disc'.

A word of warning - make sure that you have inserted the disc first - XBMC may have a meltdown if no disc has been inserted.

DI.fm and Sky.fm

If you are a music lover, then you need one, or both, of these add-ons!

DI.fm and SKY.fm are web radio stations that do nothing but stream music. And what is really great about them is that they do it by genre.

If you love the Beatles, then there is a station that only plays Beatles covers. If you love Old Skool techno, then there is a station that plays nothing but Old Skool.

DI.fm is the electronic music station. They cover everything from Drum and Bass to Goa/Psy trance and everything in between.

SKY.fm covers all the non-electronic music varieties,

including classical, metal, jazz, bollywood, rock, acoustic, country & western, Beatles, etc...

Both of these stations can be added via the XMBC.org repository from the Add-ons section of XBMC. Here is a step-by-step process for adding DI.fm (my favourite!):

1. From the main menu, go to the Setup menu in the Systems section.

2. Then go into the Add-ons section.

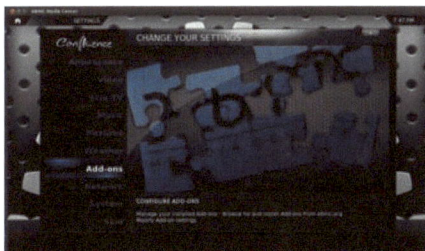

3.   Now select Get Add-ons.

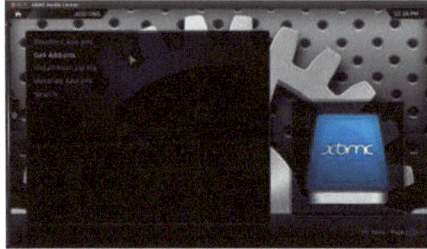

4.   Then choose the XBMC.org repository.

5.   Now select the Music Add-ons.

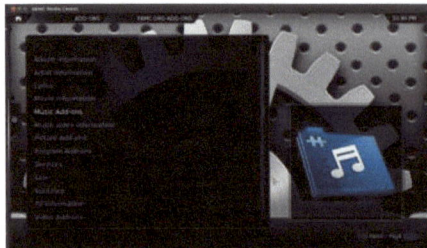

6.   Next, scroll down until you find Digitally Imported (for DI.fm) or SKY.fm and select.

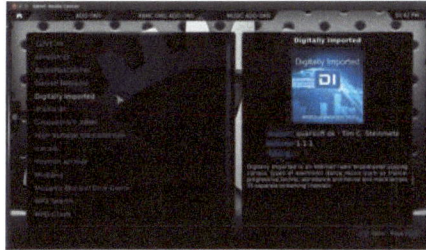

7.   Now you can install the add-on.

And you are done!

There is a configuration screen, but the only thing you will need to do here is to fill out your premium account user name and password, if you have one (this will give you no ads – not that there are many).

Repeat the above process until the last step, where you select 'Configure' to access the following screen.

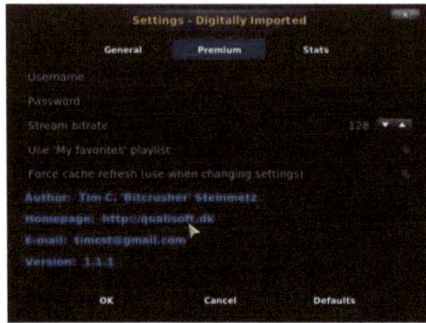

Simply fill in your details and select OK to set your premium account details.

To access the newly installed add-on, navigate to the add-on menu under the Music menu.

You can then select the "Digitally Imported" add-on.

The first time you run the add-on, it will download the stations available to you.

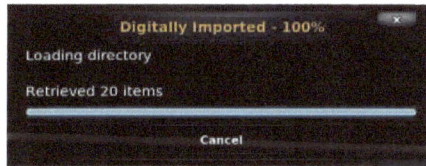

Now you can click on a genre and it will start streaming (and therefore playing) on your media centre. Nice!

And for the record, here are some of the genres available in Sky.fm:

Enjoy!

Scrappers

What on earth is a scrapper? This is a fair question. A scrapper is a program that 'scrapes' meta-data from the web about music, videos, and movies.

It does this to populate the meta-tags on the files in your collection so you can have nice wallpapers, movie covers, and artist information. Meta-tags make your media centre experience complete.

XBMC comes equipped with standard scrappers which are adequate for 90-95% of normal western content, ie: British and American movies and music.

But if you have slightly off-beat tastes, or watch a lot of non-English TV shows and movies, then you might find that the meta-data does not get populated – meaning no nice DVD covers (or CD covers either). This is where other scrappers can come into use.

So, if you like Chinese movies, you can enable a scrapper which is specifically designed to pick up meta-data for Chinese titles. There are also versions for German, French, Russian, and other Asian countries.

Installation is easy:

1.   From the main menu, go to the Setup menu in the Systems section.

2.   Then go into the Add-ons section.

3.   Now select Get Add-ons.

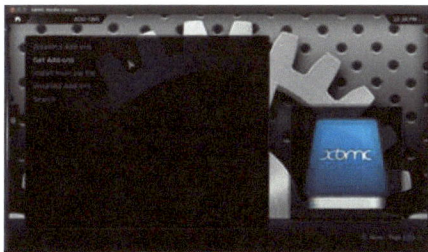

4.   Then choose the XBMC.org repository.

5.   Now select Movie Information.

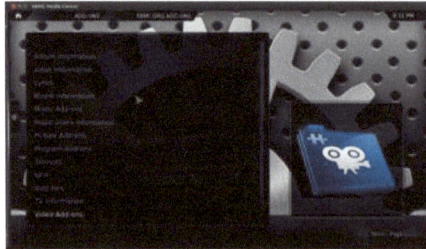

6.   Now choose your scraper. When you move over each scrapper, the right-hand window will give you a description about what each one does. In this example, I have used IMDb – the world's largest movie database. You can choose what is best for you.

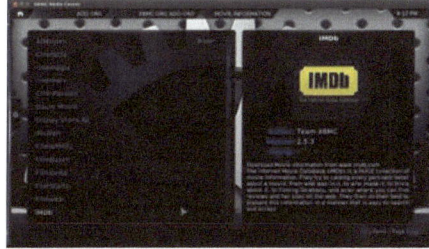

7.   The rest of the install is a process you have done before: After selecting the scrapper, a window will pop up. Press Install to install.

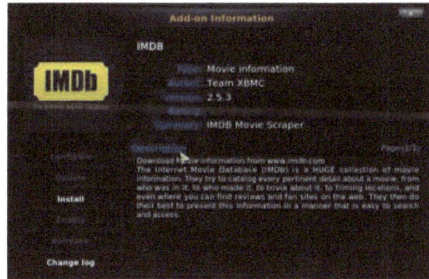

8.   Once installation is complete, you will be returned to the Movie Information Add-ons menu.

And that's it. Easy!

Now, I am not going to tell you which scrapper to use – it will depend largely on what type of content you watch. However, IMDb is a good one, especially if you watch mostly English-speaking content.

There are also scrappers for TV shows. Look in the TV Information Add-ons menu.

Music is covered by two areas: Album Information and Artist Information.

XBMC Backup

Now that you have XBMC running just the way you like it – you should back up the settings in case something goes wrong. XMBC Backup does just that. You will find it in the Program Add-ons sections of the XBMC.org repository.

Installation is the normal process – select the add-on and then choose install. There are some settings you will need to configure prior to using the add-on:

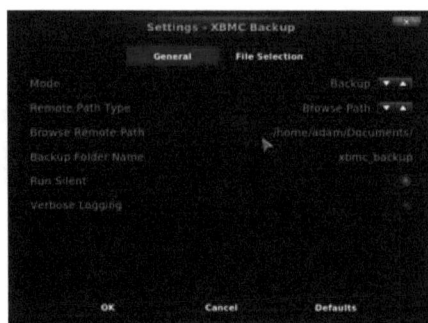

1. You will need to set a path to where the backup will be kept. This is called the "Browse Remote Path" in the settings window.

No other settings need to be changed, unless you want to.

To run the Add-on:

1. From the main menu select "Programs".

2. Then choose "XBMC Backup" and press Enter.

3.   The process will run in the background. You will not be able to move the highlighted section or cursor until this add-on has finished. When it is finished, you will be able to navigate and use the cursor again.

To restore settings that you have backed up, you need to:

1.   In the configuration of the setting (see earlier in this Add-on) change the mode to "Restore".

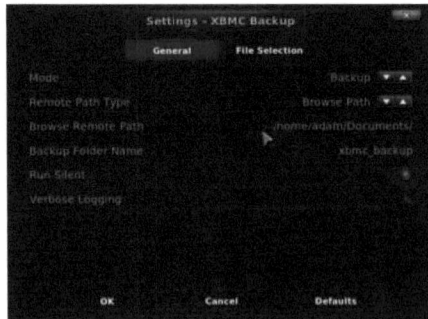

2.   Now run the add-on, as we just learned, to restore the settings.

3.   Remember to set the Mode back to Backup when you have finished restoring the XBMC configuration.

Skins

One of the big pluses that XBMC has over Windows

Media Centre is its ability to be 'skinned'. Skinning means giving the XBMC a unique look and feel, whilst retaining the core functionality of the media centre.

Skins define the look and feel of your XBMC media centre. There are a huge range of skins that you can use – but you will need to make sure that the skin meets all of your requirements – most notably Live TV.

Here is a list of skins that are confirmed to have Live TV support. Please note that this is not an exhaustive list, however it does give you a guide as to what you can successfully use as a skin with Live TV:

Aeon MQ

Aeon Nox

Cirrus Extended

Confluence *(the default skin)*

Confluence MOD

Convergence

Glass

Neon

Refocus

Transparency!

XeeBo

Not all skins have Live TV menus built into them. You have been warned :)

If you do download a skin that you decide you don't like, fear not. You can always return to the default skin.

The default skin for XBMC is Confluence – a very nice

and smooth skin. But sometime you want something a little different, or you might just not like the default skin. Luckily it is easy to change:

1. From the main menu, go to the Setup menu in the Systems section.

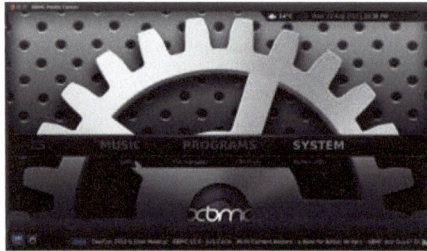

2. Then go into the Add-ons section.

3. Now select Get Add-ons.

4.   And then choose the XBMC.org repository.

5.   This time choose the Skin option.

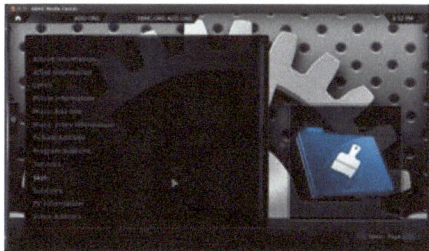

6.   Then choose a skin.

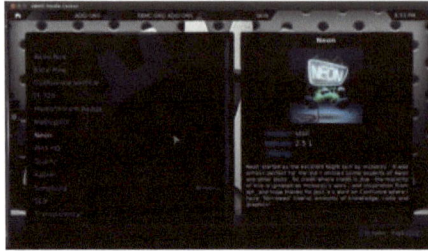

7. And then install. A word of warning – not all skins will have all the features you are looking for. Specifically check that the skin you want to install has TV support – not all of them do. You have been warned!

8. Downloading a skin can take some time, depending on your internet connection. Remember that it is downloading all the images that make up the skin.

9. When the skin has finished downloading, you will be prompted to change the skin. Obviously, you will say yes, otherwise why would you have downloaded it!?

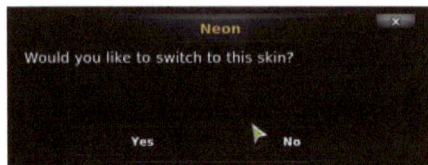

10. And voila! You have a new skin.

To change back to your old skin, or to return to the original Confluence skin:

1.   From the main menu, head to Settings under the System menu.

2.   Select the Appearance menu.

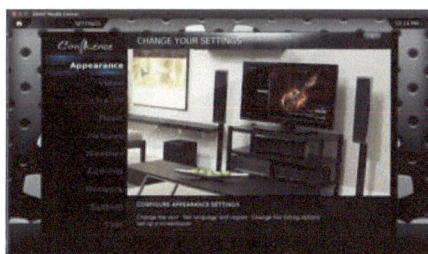

3.   In the Skin menu, select the Skin option on the right-hand window.

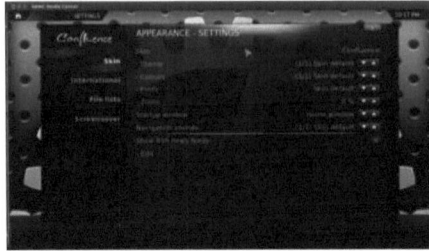

4.   Choose the Confluence skin.

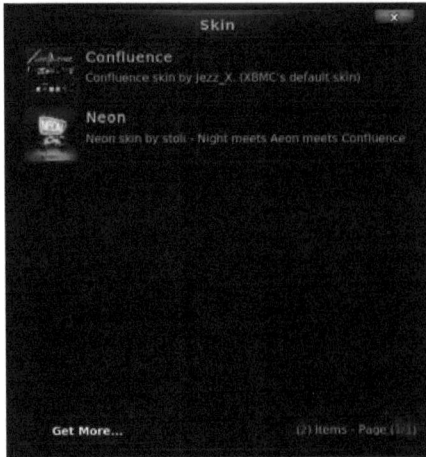

And everything goes back the way it was.

:: Wrap Up

So there you have it - you have built your first Media Centre. Congratulations!!

What you do with it is up to you. Many people's first step is to set up some 'Season Pass' recordings using the TV Guide.

A lot of people rip their CD collection so that they can listen to their favourite music and create play lists without having to risk damaging their CDs.

Some people download (legal) torrents, like the brilliant movie 'The Tunnel', and start their movie collection.

You could also start copying over your digital photos, so you can enjoy these on the big screen.

The are many possibilities ... what will you do first?

Final Words

In this book, we have addressed the issues of building and setting up your very own media centre. Arguably, the most important section of the book is the first one. Every great media centre starts with the right components. Make sure you plan your media centre. Take the time to work out what components you need and what you might want in the future.

But if you only take one thing from this book, let it be this:

Take your time.

Building a media centre is not a race. This applies particularly to the build phase. Even when setting up the software, allow yourself the time to do it slowly and methodically.

Finally, I do recommend that you check out two media centre-specific forums to find out what else you can do with your media centre:

http://www.pcmediacentre.com.au

http://www.thegreenbutton.com

PCMediacentre covers both Windows Media Centre and XBMC. There are a wide range of topics discussed, including how to tweak your media centre, how to set up an extender, and in-depth discussions on plugins and add-ons.

PCMediaCentre is an independent forum based in Australia.

The Green Button is a Microsoft forum which focuses specifically on WMC. Like the pcmediacentre.com.au site, there are a huge range of discussions on all aspects of WMC, including tweaks, tips, and plugins.

The great thing about these sites, is that the add-on and plugin developers frequent both, meaning that you will get first-hand help from the developers themselves, should you need it.

There are also a huge range of users on these forums who will have already experienced any problems you may come across, and they will have solutions. If you have any problems, these are the sites to visit.

So enjoy your media centre! Explore what it can do for you, and you will be surprised how it will change the way you consume digital media :)

:: TLA (Three Letter Acronym) Glossary

HTPC	Home Theatre PC
CPU	Central Processing Unit
GPU	Graphical Processing Unit
RAM	Random Access Memory
HDD	Hard Disc Drive
SSD	Solid State Drive (a hard drive with no moving parts)
PSU	Power Supply Unit
USB	Universal Serial Bus
PCI	Peripheral Component Interface
PCI-E	Peripheral Component Interface Express
CD	Compact Disc
DVD	Digital Video Disc
BD	Blu-ray Disc
WAF	Wife Approval Factor
SATA	Serial Advanced Technology Attachment
ATX	Advanced Technology eXtended
ITX	Information Technology eXtended
PC	Personal Computer
MHz	Mega Hertz a measurement of frequency
Cache	A special form of RAM only accessible by the CPU
LGA	Land Grid Array (a CPU socket where the pins stick up to meet contact patches on the underside of the CPU)
AMD	Advanced Micro Devices (manufacturer of CPUs)
IDE	Integrated Drive Electronics 80 Plus a PSU certification for efficiency

PAL	Phase Alternating Line (a form of analogue TV broadcasting signal)
SECAM	Séquentiel couleur à mémoire (a form of analogue TV broadcasting signal)
NTSC	National Television System Committee (a form of analogue TV broadcasting signal)
ATSC	Advanced Television Systems Committee (a form of digital TV broadcasting signal that replaced NTSC)
DVB-T	Digital Video Broadcasting Terrestrial (a form of digital TV broadcasting signal)
ISDB	Integrated Services Digital Broadcasting (a form of digital TV broadcasting signal)
DVB-S	Digital Video Broadcasting Satellite (a form of digital TV broadcasting signal)
QAM	Quadrature Amplitude Modulation (a form of digital cable TV broadcasting signal)
DDR	Double Data Rate
SDRAM	Synchronous Dynamic Random-Access Memory
IR	Infra-red
RF	Radio Frequency
DVI	Digital Visual Interface (digital video cable)
HDMI	High-Definition Multimedia Interface (digital audio visual cable)
BIOS	Basic Input Output System (system checking software used by the motherboard)
WMC	Windows Media Centre (Windows-based Media Centre software)
XBMC	XBox Media Centre (Linux-based Media Centre software)
NIC	Network Interface Card
Ubuntu	a Linux distribution ideally suited for making a media centre